The Art of
Teaching Reading:
A Language and
Self-Concept
Approach

The Charles E. Merrill
COMPREHENSIVE READING PROGRAM

Arthur Heilman
Consulting Editor

The Art of Teaching Reading: A Language and Self-Concept Approach

Hope W. Dunne
Northern Michigan University

CHARLES E. MERRILL PUBLISHING COMPANY
A Bell & Howell Company
Columbus, Ohio

Published by
Charles E. Merrill Publishing Co.
A Bell & Howell Company
Columbus, Ohio 43216

International Standard Book Number: 0-675-09075-x

Library of Congress Catalog Card Number: 72-80163

1   2   3   4   5   6   7   8   9   10—76   75   74   73   72

PRINTED IN THE UNITED STATES OF AMERICA

*To my father's tenacity and
my mother's sensitivity to
the needs of people*

In Memory Of

Harrison and Willa Willcutts

Foreword

Past and present practices in attempting to teach all children to read printed materials have produced less than desirable results. Many problems are apparent. Hope Dunne in *The Art of Teaching Reading: A Language and Self-Concept Approach,* has attempted, and succeeded, in guiding teachers to some basic solutions to reading. She has highlighted the child's view of himself as a prime consideration during the process of acquiring reading skills and abilities. She has linked language development to reading through the emphasis on experience units. The methods and materials which result lead teachers away from the practice of engaging children in an endless round of trying to find and remember millions of answers to questions they did not ask. Her suggestions are not sterilized and prepackaged. They are open to the experience background and the home-rooted language of each learner. They depend on interaction and participation of children and adults.

In this book, the learning to read process is launched from a few questions which persist throughout life. Some of them are:

"Who am I?"

"What can I do?"

"What can I observe and hear in my world?"

"How is what I observe and hear related to the print I see?"

"How can I find out about what other people have thought about and said?"

"What is in my imaginary world—the world that I can never experience *really?*"

Finding answers to these questions makes possible enjoyment, appreciation, and internalization of the creative thinking of thousands of people. Life and language are extended. Art and life are integrated. Speech and print are unified and inseparable. A human being is reading because he is answering significant questions which he has asked himself.

Roach Van Allen

University of Arizona

Preface

The public has been made keenly aware of the problems of our schools by John Holt's three books—HOW CHILDREN LEARN; HOW CHILDREN FAIL; THE UNDERACHIEVING SCHOOL. More recently Charles E. Silberman has written CRISIS IN THE CLASSROOM. Concerned discussion about the teaching of reading, in particular, takes place among people in social gatherings everywhere. It is generally recognized that the high rate of physical and psychological dropout in later grades can be traced to the degree of success a child experiences in learning to read in the early primary grades. The damage done to the self-concept of a child who encounters failure in learning to read, is difficult to overcome by remedial teaching. A positive, preventive program is needed.

The purpose of this book is to give classroom teachers a "blueprint" for making learning to read a relevant and successful experience for each child *from the very first day* of school. The art of pacing and challenging a child through inductive teaching is detailed. As the child "grows into reading" he will be discovering and contributing to the total learning process of the room at his level of development—in his unique way. Techniques for guiding the child in self-selection and in planning his time are described. Unit teaching in a self-contained classroom provides the framework.

Successful experiences are superficial unless reinforced with skill development. This book aids a teacher in the diagnostic teaching of skills. Specific ideas are given for use in the listening center to individualize instruction for development of independence in reading. All skill development is linguistically based.

The ideas in this book have been tested in the classroom not only by myself, but by successful, experienced teachers who have found them to be both practical and effective. Classroom management, as described herein, frees the teacher to help the children who need it most. Ultimately, it makes it possible for all to be creative and productive as they plan together in carrying forth an integrated school curriculum. Continuous pupil progress is the result.

I am currently using this program in the training of prospective classroom teachers at Northern Michigan University. This book will be particularly helpful to college professors who need a detailed program for students in language-arts and reading methods classes for use in laboratory teaching. All of the case material demonstrating children's work, except that in Chapter Five, has come from my students' experiences with heterogeneous groups of five or six children in a regular classroom.

It is hoped that the positive program detailed in this book will help to further:

1. Preservice professional training in teacher-training institutions.
2. Inservice training of classroom teachers.
3. Implementation of innovative ideas within the school.
4. Leadership of educators to enlist the community in *meaningful* involvement. Schools must become the center of community life.

Hope W. Dunne

Acknowledgments

Grateful acknowledgment is made of the inspiration and insight gained from personal contacts with Roach Van Allen, Peggy Brogan, Bill Martin, Jr., Newell Kephart, Russell Stauffer, Walter Barbe, Helen Murphy, Donald Durrell, William K. Durr, and Harry Hahn. Clifford H. Smart,* former superintendent of the Walled Lake Michigan School District gave me my first opportunity, as reading coordinator, to incorporate their philosophies into the implementation of my own. As reading coordinator I was able to develop the program described in this book with the aid of creative classroom teachers of the school district.

I am especially indebted to Thomas Culhane, former principal of the John D. Pierce Laboratory School, Northern Michigan University, and his first- and second-grade teachers who allowed me to initiate my laboratory project there for preservice training of teachers. I wish to give my warmest thanks to the fine administrators and teachers of the public and parochial schools of Marquette, Michigan, who have made it possible for me to expand the laboratory classroom program. And to all of my Northern Michigan University students during the past four years who have worked so hard and contributed so much through their laboratory work, I express my gratitude for their willingness to have me use material they developed.

I wish to pay tribute to all who have given me editorial help as I have struggled to put all of the details down: Alverta Koplin, Marty

---

* Currently a member of the Education Committee of the Michigan House of Representatives.

Bush, Kathleen Dunne Tyree, Sandra Dent, Stewart Kingsbury, and Joan Potvin.

There are many whom I should thank. I have left to the end the one to whom I owe the most, my husband. He has patiently assisted me in these two difficult years of writing and rewriting.

Hope W. Dunne

Contents

The Art of
Teaching Reading:
A Language and
Self-Concept
Approach

CHAPTER ONE

Identifying
the Problem

An era that has left an imprint of man's footsteps on the moon should be capable of updating its schools so that each child finds a learning environment which accepts and encourages his individuality. With such rapid advancement in technology, parents realize that their children's future ability to compete depends upon the acquisition of learning skills based on the "three Rs"—reading, 'riting, and 'rithmetic. How else can their children attain all of the knowledge needed, not only to *compete* in today's world, but to help *solve* its vast problems!

This technological advancement has had an impact upon publishing companies and, in turn, upon schools. "New" methods of teaching communication skills (speaking, listening, writing, and reading) and mathematics bombard teachers and parents with unfamiliar, sometimes perplexing, terms and techniques that often appear threatening and contradictory, rather than challenging.

THE CHILD AS A LEARNER

The findings and research reflected early in the twentieth century in the philosophy of John Dewey (3) and Marie Montessori (8), unfortunately, have *not* been put into practice in most of our classrooms. Their emphasis was upon the child as the learner with need for him to explore and experience his environment in a meaningful way. Although noted child psychologists (2, 9) and educators have worked to develop Dewey's and Montessori's philosophy further, most schools continue to operate in a manner contradictory to these teachings.

1

Nevertheless, the knowledge that neurological (5, 6) and maturational (4) development patterns differ greatly among children has been re-emphasized in recent years. This re-emphasis has caused educators to become increasingly aware of individual differences within the classroom. As far back as 1946, Dr. Emmet Betts recognized a need to acknowledge beginning readers as individuals when he said:

> The highest level of teaching is the unified language-experience approach; attractive library tables with books for browsing; a variety of trade books supplementary to curriculum and recreational reading; basal textbooks in all school subjects used primarily as reference; basal workbooks used to meet specific needs of pupils . . . (1).

This need for individualizing was further developed during the fifties, based upon Dr. Willard Olson's concepts of child growth and development:

> *Self-seeking*—Each child makes an active exploration of his environment.
>
> *Self-selection*—Each child selects the environment (learning materials) appropriate to his needs.
>
> *Self-pacing*—In reading, pacing deals with the development of skills and interest at the rate of the child, rather than at some predetermined rate which is applied either to the entire class or to some artificial grouping. The teacher has the responsibility to provide materials which the child can thrive upon at his level of maturity (7).

When this process of learning succeeds, it focuses on the child as a learner. Instead of the child being made to "fit" into an instructional system, the educational program is organized to meet his individual needs. It is through this kind of development that the child understands and achieves. The teacher assists the child in his search for relevant experiences, inspires interest, provides a wealth of reading material at the child's instructional level, and insures diagnostic teaching through daily individual teacher-pupil conferences. The important result of this interaction is that the child develops in communication skills as he feels success as an individual.

Homogeneous Grouping—An Administrative Attempt to Meet Individual Differences

The concept of pacing, however, has led most school administrators and teachers to plan programs based upon homogeneous grouping of children in relation to their growth patterns, e.g., maturation, perceptual-motor development. They have felt that homogeneous grouping is the most efficient and effective way to handle differences among children. Structured teaching of reading has resulted, in which one of the following forms of classroom organization is used:

1. Three homogeneous reading groups within the classroom—low, middle, and high.

2. Cross-class grouping for reading (sometimes called the Joplin Plan) which sends children to different rooms at a certain time of the day for homogeneous teaching of reading, e.g., a first-grade child going to the third grade for the reading period or vice versa.

3. "Multiple track" classroom system within a particular grade—used in larger school systems. Children are assigned to self-contained classrooms according to their readiness or reading level determined by achievement tests.

All of these organizational plans have been designed with a sincere desire to meet individual differences, but they have overlooked the fact that each child has different characteristics and needs, which predetermined learning and homogeneous grouping alone fail to meet. The key to operating this type of a classroom is the placement of children according to a standardized reading test. These tests, however, do not reveal individual needs. By using reading scores as a basis for grouping (the "easy way" administratively), an intrinsic element of the entire process is overlooked—*the child's self-concept!* Children separated in such a manner soon get the idea: you're dumb, I'm smart, you're in-between! How many times have teachers heard or observed this from children, either in words or actions? The action may take the form of either withdrawal or disruptive behavior, which are both detrimental to learning.

What is Self-Concept?

Self-concept is the feeling within the child that he can "conquer the world." Nurturing such a feeling requires a school environment which:

1. Helps him to overcome problems arising from his sociological and/or psychological background. (While the teacher must be aware of deficiencies in the child's background, he must never use this knowledge as an excuse for an inadequate approach to the child's problems. Teacher statements such as, "I can't do

anything with Johnny because . . ." are statements of the non-professional.)

2. Helps him to succeed in relationship to his maturation patterns.

3. Respects his individuality and encourages peer acceptance.

4. Challenges and inspires him to further intellectual growth.

Unstructuring the Classroom

In 1963, this writer was privileged to hear Dr. Helen Murphy of Boston University. The following statements are paraphrased from her speech:*

The first day of school is the most important.

Reading achievement in later grades is related to the success or failure of the child on the first day of school in the first grade!

A teacher's idea of an immature child is one who does not do what the teacher thinks he should do at the time the teacher has planned it should be done.

No mental age guarantees success, it is the way the child is taught.

Since listening to this dynamic educator, the writer has been striving to find practical answers to teaching reading to the primary child while simultaneously protecting his self-concept.** This book is the result of that effort and will deal forthrightly with two basic problems of the classroom:

1. Protection of the child's SELF-CONCEPT as an individual functioning in a democratic society.

2. Description of a program that will enable *each child's learning to be relevant and continuous.*

What kind of concrete program can be offered to make it possible for children to develop according to their growth patterns without injuring their self-concept? Chapter Two will deal specifically with practical

---

* Permission granted by Dr. Murphy for paraphrasing from her speech.

**Practical public school experience has included seven years of classroom teaching and three year's work as a reading consultant in the Walled Lake School District, Oakland County, Michigan. During this period, the writer participated in a project with Dr. Harry Hahn, Oakland University, director of "A Study of the Relative Effectiveness of Three Methods of Teaching Reading in Grade One," Project #2687, U.S. Office of Education, 1964-66.

ideas for such a program, one which will aim at preventing "dropouts" the very first day of school. In order to make certain that the ideas and methods are practical, they have been discussed in detail with first- and second-grade teachers who, in turn, have put them into operation in their classrooms.

The techniques have more recently been tested by the writer and by other primary teachers who have been willing to "unstructure" their classrooms and convert them into "learning laboratories." In such an atmosphere, children are allowed self-selection, and they view each other as equals. One such teacher* has unstructured her classroom. She does not intend to wait again until April to get children cooperatively involved in the learning process but intends to start the very first day of school! Yet, she feels that teachers who have taught in a structured organization, as well as new teachers, need to have very detailed help for starting this type of instruction. While Chapter Two deals primarily with the first grade, the ideas can be adapted for use in any of the grades.

REFERENCES

1. Betts, Emmet A. *Foundations of Reading Instruction.* New York: American Book Co., 1946.

2. Bruner, Jerome S. *Toward a Theory of Instruction.* Cambridge: The Belknap Press, 1966.

3. Dewey, John. *The School and Society.* Chicago: The University of Chicago Press, 1899.

4. Ilg, Frances L., and Ames, Louise Bates. *School Readiness.* New York: Harper and Row, 1965.

5. Kephart, Newell C. *The Slow Learner in the Classroom.* Columbus, Ohio: Charles E. Merrill Publishing Co., 1960, 1971.

6. McLeod, Pierce. *Readiness for Learning.* New York: J. B. Lippincott Co., 1965.

7. Olson, Willard, C. *Child Development.* Boston: D. C. Heath and Co., 1949.

8. Orem, R. C., ed. *A Montessori Handbook.* New York: Capricorn Books, 1966.

9. Phillips, John L., Jr. *The Origins of Intellect: Piaget's Theory.* San Francisco: W. H. Freeman and Company, 1969.

* Mary Ellen Wollenberg, a first-grade teacher.

SUPPLEMENTARY REFERENCES

Anderson, Verna Dieckman. *Reading and Young Children*. New York: The Macmillan Company, 1968.

Austin, David; Clark, Velma; and Fitchett, Gladys. *Reading Rights for Boys; Sex Role in Language Experience*. New York: Appleton-Century-Crofts, 1971.

Purkey, William W. *Self-Concept and School Achievement*. Englewood Cliffs, New Jersey: Prentice-Hall, Inc., 1970.

CHAPTER TWO

Success for Each Child— Starting the First Day of School

The tone is set *on the first day* of school for the kind of learning experiences that are going to take place in the classroom throughout the year. No matter which grade is being taught, the happenings on that first day can kindle or smother enthusiasm for learning. Each child is tired of vacation and goes to school that first day hoping to be caught up in an exciting and meaningful experience. This is a most important day, also, for the teacher to begin diagnostic observations.

MAKING EACH CHILD FEEL IMPORTANT

While the program that follows is detailed primarily for kindergarteners and first graders, the ideas, with modification, will adapt to any grade. Parenthetical comments will be made to suggest ideas for such adaptation for higher grades.

Since most children come to the first grade thinking they are going to read the very first day of school, teachers must protect such anticipation by discovering ways to satisfy this desire and by dealing with each child as a unique individual—with a need to feel good about himself. Based upon these objectives, a typical first day plan should include the utilization of name cards for each child, the association of the alphabet with children's names, the introduction of choral reading, the inspiration of authorship, the reading of stories, and a start toward each child's personal collection of interesting words.

7

PREPARING EACH DESK IN ADVANCE

Advance preparation is required to equip each child's desk as an activity center for the day. Begin by taping a card with a child's name written in manuscript at the top of each desk to be discovered by the proper child and viewed as he sits down. If possible, provide a copy of *Sounds of Home* (7). Teachers unfamiliar with this text will find that it provides delightful ways to fill children's ears with sounds of language patterns through the use of appealing literary selections. Colorful pictures and often unique print help readers see what they hear. If this text is not available, an interesting picture book should be on every desk along with a piece of drawing paper, a pencil, and some crayons. These provisions will help to prevent restlessness while all children are being assembled, since it takes time to get a group into their respective desks in readiness for the first activity.

(*For older children,* no name cards will be placed on desks in advance, but drawing paper, pencil, and crayons are essential. Interesting trade and library books should be on each desk also. Books relating to the first unit study would be most appropriate. These books will not necessarily relate to the child's reading achievement on the first day. The classroom teacher should have a bulletin board, partially developed, on the unit of study which is to be introduced the *very first day,* e.g., social studies, science. From the stimulation of the bulletin board and the books on each desk, the child should be encouraged to use the drawing paper to make illustrations to complete the bulletin board.)

USING NAME CARDS

As the kindergartener or first grader enters the classroom for the first time, he will be directed to a table where he is to find his own name card to wear. In order to speed this operation, double-stick tape is placed on the back of each card. Then, he is instructed to find his desk, identified by a matching name card. Teachers should work out a plan for children to re-use these cards until they know the children's names automatically.

(*For older children,* blank cards, appropriate to be made into name cards, should be picked up by each as he arrives. Wearing name cards is essential for easy identification of children at first, regardless of grade level. A teacher can learn a great deal from the way each child prints or writes his name and decorates his card. Allow these children to seat themselves—at first—as they wish.)

ASSOCIATING THE ALPHABET WITH FIRST
GRADERS' AND KINDERGARTENERS' NAMES

A chalkboard exercise, prepared beforehand, can be used in introducing the children to the alphabet:

A	Agnes, Ann	J	Jerry, Joan	S	Sally, Sam
B	Barbara	K	Karen, Kevin	T	Tom
C	Carl, Cathy	L	Larry	U	
D	Debbie, Douglas	M	Mary	V	Virginia
E	Earl, Edna	N	Ned	W	Warren, William
F	Fred	O	Oliver	X	
G	Gary	P	Pam, Perry	Y	Yvonne
H	Helen	Q		Z	
I		R	Ralph		

When the children are settled at their desks wearing their name cards, the teacher can call attention to the letters and names written on the board. Since most children know the alphabet song, it can be used in introducing them to each other as well as giving each recognition as the song is sung. They can be told to stand and sing the song while first looking at the chalkboard arrangement. The second time it is sung, each will sit down as the letter is sung that starts his name.* This kind of opening exercise might be enjoyed for three or four mornings by kindergarteners and first graders *only*.

In addition to making children feel good about themselves, this activity serves as an introduction to sounds related to letters—a most important beginning skill needed for reading.

INTRODUCING CHORAL READING

Full use of language is fundamental to later success in reading as none of the communication skills can develop as isolated parts, but all must unfold as a continuous, interrelated whole. Choral reading can be used to initiate this process the first day of school. It can be started by

---

* Plan suggested by Dr. Helen Murphy, Boston University. Permission granted for its use.

the teacher having the children gather on the floor** around her to sing nursery rhymes that have been set to music. One particular nursery rhyme, set to music, that has proven very successful for this purpose is "Three Blind Mice." Children must be given the idea that choral reading is like singing a song together—no one rushes ahead.

(*For second graders and above,* singing the song "Row Row Row Your Boat"—in rounds—is a good opener for choral reading. The poetry to be used should be appropriate for introducing the unit of study.)

After the singing, the teacher can read a simple poem to kindergarteners and first graders. If a set of *Sounds of Home* is provided for their use, the children should have been told to bring them for the choral reading activity. Then they can follow along with the teacher as she reads any selection the children and the teacher may decide upon together. However, from other sets of books available, simple poems can be read. The point is that for kindergarteners and first graders a book should be used. For some children there will be an association between sound and symbol, and thus reading is started easily. For others, it may be just memorization, but it satisfies the first grader's desire to hold and read a book—the very first day.

To make choral reading successful, markers, which can be made from construction paper cut to size, should be used to place under each line being read. For kindergarteners and first graders these markers should be the same size as the page upon which they are used. Many children's eyes have not stabilized at this age. Unless the marker extends to the bottom of the page read, it may not help keep the child's eyes on the line being read.

ENCOURAGING CHILDREN TO WRITE

Another idea to be established on the first day of school is that each child can be an author! This first experience with authorship requires that the teacher make careful preparation. For it to be successful with kindergarteners and first graders, the teacher can place the following materials on a table for the children to file by and collect:

** Reluctance to sit on the floor, soiled by the tracking in of children on rainy and/or snowy days, can be resolved by the use of "sitting seats." This idea provides an art project for children as well as a phoneme-grapheme alliteration experience with /s/. For ease and durability, strong brown grocery sacks can be decorated and labeled: e.g., John's sitting seat sack. A creative teacher can devise many other ways of making them.

1. One large sheet of colored construction paper.

2. A white sheet of paper upon which the following has been dittoed—I am _____.

The first two words, "I am," will have been done in proper manuscript with dashes so that the child can trace over the three letters connecting the dashes and then write his own name on the blank line, using the name card on his desk as a guide. There will be enough space under this line for him to draw a picture of himself. As the children work on this project, the teacher can circulate throughout the room and write one simple sentence which each child dictates about himself.

(*For older children,* authorship will be related to activities stimulated from choral reading and visual aids which introduce the first unit of study.)

PREPARING A BOOKLET FOR THE FIRST STORY

The child is told to fold his large sheet of construction paper in half *with the fold placed on the left side.* An activity requiring kindergarteners and first graders to raise left and right hands will have to take place for them to understand these directions. This gives the teacher an opportunity to mentally single out those who are going to need a great deal of help in recognizing left and right. A good way for the teacher to have made provision for the many children who will have this difficulty is to have a drawing of the left hand and the right hand taped to the appropriate side of each child's desk with left *or* right printed on the drawings. Beginning and ending consonants should be underlined: left, right. Later, children can outline their left and right hands and compare them with the ones on their desks.

Children with coordination problems are not going to be able to fold their construction paper evenly.* Uneven covers can be straightened as the teacher staples their first stories into booklets *to be taken home, the very first day!* Each child prints his name once again, as it is pointed out that the author's name is usually written at the bottom of the front book cover.

---

* This often indicates that finger dexterity needed for good penmanship is lacking. The teacher should make mental note of these children. Future planning for them should include activities designed to develop coordination and strengthen small muscles of the hand needed to gain control over tools used in writing, e.g., putting puzzles together, cutting with scissors, finger painting, clay modeling, using crayons for drawing.

RECOGNIZING ATTENTION SPAN

The teacher will have to be very conscious of attention span, particularly at first. A teacher must be prepared with interesting games and/or physical exercises that will involve listening and also be an outlet for the children's abundant physical energy (6). Be prepared to do something to take care of restlessness at least every twenty minutes, at first, involving all of the children. In this way discipline problems are *prevented from the very first day.* If enough physical activity is part of the routine schedule, children can be taught to respect the requirement of order at other times so that all can learn. This does not necessarily imply that children be required to sit at their desks; it simply means that each must be taught to move around the room to get supplies, books, etc., in a manner that is not distracting.

READING TO THE CHILDREN

Using a story with large, interesting illustrations, the teacher begins reading to the children the first day. It is important to show them the pictures and encourage response and interaction to what is being read. The selected story should lend itself to thought-provoking discussion which is the beginning of critical thinking. The first step should be taken to help the child understand what is expected of him as a member of such a group. Dr. James Moffett says, as a child wants

> to talk he does not raise his hand; his cue to speaking is someone else's stopping. One of the main problems of the teacher-led discussion is that children tend to talk to the teacher instead of to each other. If the teacher calls on children who raise their hands, the teacher inevitably becomes the focus of the group, which is difficult to avoid in any case since he is being directive in other ways. A rule about hearing out the last speaker and then starting to speak without signaling will help children to focus on each other and reinforce the rule about listening (8).

Since taking turns is one of the main objectives in social living in the classroom, the above quote from Dr. Moffett offers a goal to strive for, one that will require teacher direction at first. It will be accomplished as the children find that the climate of the room is one where they are involved with the teacher in planning learning activities. This will not eliminate the necessity at certain times throughout the day for the children to listen attentively to the teacher.

COLLECTING PERSONAL WORDS

When stories are read, the children should be asked if any new or interesting words are heard. This question usually elicits prompt responses. As each child says the word, the teacher prints it on a card for him. The teacher suggests that each class member may want to keep a word file of interesting words he hears and sees in reading. Fulfillment of this activity requires the teacher:

1. To have a large supply of 4 x 5 inch filing cards available for use (this size card is just wide enough to stand upright in a shoe box).
2. To be prepared with a brightly colored magic marker for printing words on cards.
3. To set aside each child's collection of words until the next day when shoe boxes can be decorated to "house" them.

Since word study can be related to such word collections, many learning possibilities can evolve from this practice. A few examples are learning consonants in initial, terminal, and medial positions; alphabetizing; categorizing—letting each child use his own thinking process to figure out ways to classify words; developing word vocabulary, correctly spelled, to which the children, as "authors," may refer. Once the plan gets into operation, the creative teacher, with the help of the children, will think of many additional ways for using the cards.

REVIEWING THE OBJECTIVES

Perhaps at this point a summary and review should be made of how to set the stage for developing a learning laboratory atmosphere on the very first day.

1. Each child is treated as an equal; therefore, homogeneous grouping is not considered as a part of the classroom organization, except for word study.

2. A natural start is made on the development of auditory and visual discrimination of consonant sounds—the teacher and the children should start immediately to underline all consonants in words.

   a. A list of the children's names left on a chalk or bulletin board for several days will offer an opportunity for associating initial and ending consonant sounds with beginning and final letters.

   b. Children begin to learn the phonemes /l/ and /r/ in initial position and /t/ in final position by observing the words "left" and "right."*

   c. Important objects in the classroom can be labeled by the teacher and used to teach beginning and ending consonant sounds rather than be dealt with simply as sight words (4, 9).

3. Choral reading is established as a very important part of the day's activities.

   a. This activity can be used for language development as it is initially learned.

   b. With simple poems committed to memory, choral speaking can be utilized to keep order "in the line" as children prepare to file to and from classes, etc.

   c. Choral reading or choral speaking can relieve tension and restore room control when restlessness begins.

4. The idea of authorship is introduced.

5. Children are helped to grow into reading by listening and reacting to stories.

6. A basis for a word study program is established by beginning a collection of personal words.

7. Physical exercises are started with major emphasis upon developing the concept of "left" and "right" (6).

---

* Sound-letter association (phoneme-grapheme relationship) has more meaning to children when it is gained from a personal concrete experience. Thus, having children hold up a crayon whose color name is pronounced, then printed—for introduction of an initial consonant or blend—makes phoneme-grapheme development real: i.e., red, purple, or yellow crayon for the sound represented by the *r, p,* or *y;* black, green or gray for the sound represented by the letters *bl* or *gr.* Reinforcement of a particular sound can be done with alliteration exercises. Use of concrete objects, pictures drawn or cut out—assembled with each sound-letter relationship to be developed—can become the basis for a dictated story. Example: Robert Robin Redbreast runs along the road.

All of these activities will be continued in some form on a daily basis. However, on the second day of school, reading and a word study program should also be started.

READING

A teacher's first concern in making preparations for the reading program will be to gather a sufficient number of adequate books to be placed attractively on a reading table or in a reading center. For kindergarteners and first graders, suitable books should include basal pre-primers and primers, along with trade books* written at a level no higher than the first grade. Interesting picture books should be included.

With a wealth of appropriate reading material available to him, each child is encouraged to browse through the books, select one, and keep it at his desk until it has been "read." Since he is told that he will be given an opportunity to discuss his book with the teacher that day, he should be ready with a book. With an understanding that reading can be talking about pictures, the child will not become concerned with the fact that he is unable to figure out the words at this point. *The teacher's attitude about what constitutes reading is important* and will keep him from feeling afraid to select a picture book for his reading.

(*For children in second grade and above,* the basal reader, social studies, and/or science text books at grade level should be used in the reading circle for a fast class survey of individual reading achievement. The child will read orally to the teacher *only.* This will allow the teacher to learn quickly the word recognition ability of each child without damaging self-confidence. Techniques for this are discussed further in Chapter Three under individualized reading.)

Grouping Heterogeneously

Most classrooms have approximately thirty children. Efficient room operation, as well as personalized diagnostic teaching, requires dividing the children into groups. The pupils should be involved in this organiza-

---

* Trade books follow the principle of controlled vocabulary for beginning readers or for older children with low reading achievement. In recent years, book companies have been increasing the supply of delightful books for independent reading for all children in such areas as fiction, science, biography, travel. Examples: *Let's Read and Find Out Books,* New York: Thomas Y. Crowell Co., 1962-1963; Eva Knox Witte, *American Biographies,* New York: Holt, Rinehart and Winston, Inc., 1968.

tion, forming teams to provide for working in groups. This can be done with a minimum of confusion if three sheets of chart paper are taped at eye-level height on the chalkboard. Each will have a heading: Team I, Team II, and Team III. Along the left-hand side of the chart, the numerals one to ten will be listed, assuming there are thirty children in the room. It will be explained to the children that each can decide which team he wants to join. After deciding, he will be instructed to write his name beside a numeral on the chart; no more can be on any one team than there are numerals. The result will probably be a room organized into three heterogeneous groups.

I want to read with
Team I
1. Randy Wilson
2. Sherrie Conner
3. Bert M...

1. Ma)
2.
3.
4
5.
6.
7
8.

Child signing up for chosen team

Providing children with an opportunity to choose their group undoubtedly will have a resemblance of friendship grouping. This is a good way to start the year as it will be a deterrent to the loneliness and fear of many children that so often interferes with early classroom adjustment. It also will be placing responsibility upon each child to help with room organization.

At an appropriate time, Team I is called to the reading circle. The teacher's *daily* schedule must be so designed that *all three teams are called in the same day.* At first, an attempt should be made to get each pupil to take a turn *talking* to the entire group about a favorite page from the book he has chosen to "read." Of course, it must be realized that only a few actually will be able to read their books in kindergarten and first grade.

If it is possible to get all of the children in the team to participate as a group at such an early stage, the teacher can advance immediately to the method of operation that will serve as the format for all ensuing sessions. The teacher will work with and give undivided attention to the child sitting next to him—*on a rotating basis*—with the other children occupying themselves independently, *looking at or reading* their books. Thus, only one child at a time will share his lesson with the teacher by discussing a picture or reading a selected page. In this way, individual teacher-pupil conferences are established. Each must be brief, not taking over two minutes for each child, as the group reading period should not last over twenty minutes, at first. During this time, each child must be encouraged to "read" quietly to the teacher so as not to distract the others who will learn to "read" to themselves until their turn with the teacher. While this is the goal, it may take as long as two or three weeks to accomplish it with first graders. Older children will catch on to this organization more quickly.

As the teacher listens to one child at a time, a record of the pupil's errors and successes is started. A 5 x 8 inch index card for each child can be utilized for this important record keeping, which will lead to diagnostic teaching. Later, it will serve as the guide for word study grouping which will be *homogeneous.*

Providing Independent Work for the Other Teams During the Reading Period

What will the other children be doing during the three different reading periods? At the beginning of the year, creative art will help to motivate the child to express his individuality as well as to develop his coordination. Ideas for art work will evolve as the children pursue a unit of study. Later, meaningful seatwork activities will be provided in accordance with the child's need for skill development. For example, page 21 describes seatwork activities correlating manuscript, word study, and writing for kindergarteners and first graders.

MEANINGFUL ART ACTIVITIES AT THE "MAKE-IT" TABLE

A "make-it" table (3) is an ideal means of developing interest and imagination in art work. A table should be placed in a specified area of the room and equipped with a variety of materials. While the teacher may want to furnish such basic items as construction paper, crayons, and glue, the children should be encouraged to collect and bring in whatever materials they feel could be useful at the "make-it" table, e.g., egg cartons, buttons, wooden boxes, different sized cans. Then, as one group is reading, the other children can work quietly on their individual or group creations!

A project related to the word collections provides the first meaningful art activity for them. To implement this task, the teacher must have collected enough empty shoe boxes so that one will be available for each child to store his word cards. Each child will decorate his shoe box with construction paper or paint, according to his individuality. Since paste or painting will be used for this activity, children will have to be taught to use them carefully and to put newspaper on their desks beforehand to keep them clean. Once minor instructions of this type are given, the children should be left to develop their own creations.

Class members can help each other in placing construction paper on the boxes. One of the outstanding advantages of heterogeneous grouping is that children learn to assist each other, and the teacher is freed to direct other lessons.

For identifying each box, the teacher can have dittoed 4 x 6 inch forms upon which the following can be placed in dashed manuscript for the child to trace over: Words I Like. Then, after the child prints his name under this sentence, the card will be pasted on the front of the box. Each child can be encouraged to decorate and identify his box in accordance with his own individuality.

(*For older children,* smaller boxes appropriate for 3 x 5 inch cards can be used. Using 3 x 5 inch cards allows for a flexible word study program, e.g., the reverse side of the card can be used to write a simple sentence containing the "personal" word—underlining it—to reinforce later recognition.)

MANUSCRIPT PREPARATION

The "make-it" table activities can be splendid preparation for manuscript for kindergarteners and first graders. Finger coordination can be developed here. Circles, straight lines (sticks), and arcs are the important basic forms the children must be able to make in order to write. A teacher should use his imagination, as well as a manual on teaching manuscript, to help children make these forms properly. Use of clay is a good medium. Children can make circles and "sticks" out of clay and put them together for such letters as *d, b, p, l,* manuscript *a,* etc. Or they can try cutting big circles and "sticks" out of paper to make these letters. Maybe they will want to draw them first and then cut them. After they have practiced making letters for awhile, they can make interesting animals or other objects out of clay. All of this is good for developing finger dexterity.

Examples of Other Activities for the "Make-it" Table

Sheets of white construction paper, crayons, scissors, paste, buttons, and small scraps of colorful cloth can be provided for an art activity in which children create cloth pictures related to a unit under study. They can draw a picture on a piece of construction paper (e.g., an animal, a person) and paste small pieces of fabric (already cut by the teacher for kindergarteners and first graders) to fill in the picture outlines. These pictures can later become the basis for writing (dictating) a story.

As children become authors by writing independently or by dictating to the teacher, they will produce stories from which booklets can be made. Each team can be taught to make hard-back covers* and to decorate them. Team members are encouraged to help each other. This will be possible after the teacher has taken sufficient time to instruct the whole class in the process of bookmaking.

Instructing the class in making hard book covers

Unit study themes, which are discussed in Chapters Three and Four, will give rise to many independent and meaningful art activities, e.g., murals, posters.

---

* See appendix, page 143, for instructions on making hard-back covers.

LISTENING CENTER

A corner of the room must be equipped as a listening center. A record player and tape recorder with microphone and headphones* will aid in the development of many important language skills independent of the teacher. Using headphones, six children at a time can participate quietly in meaningful learning while the teacher is meeting with other groups. For example:

1. Listening to stories (either on records or teacher-prepared tapes) without a conclusion can motivate them to write or illustrate the ending.

2. Listening to teacher-prepared tapes made to accompany the exercises in the Durrell-Murphy Phonics Practice Kit,** or other prepared phonics material, reinforces the visual. Without this auditory association with the visual, the phonic skills are not fully developed.

3. Listening to teacher-prepared tapes on grade level science and social textbooks, the underachieving child, following the text, is not only aided in reading skill development, but acquires an understanding of the facts under discussion in the classroom.

Individual use of the microphone provides the teacher with a recording of a child's natural language patterns for diagnostic purposes. It is invaluable to use in giving the Informal Reading Inventory (see appendix, page 149).

The Listening Center will become an increasingly valuable means for individualizing instruction as children's problems are *daily* diagnosed.

WORD STUDY PROGRAM

The word study program should begin informally with the entire class in all grades.

The following detailed program is described for kindergarteners and first graders. It is based upon a concept stressed by Drs. Durrell and Murphy in their *Speech-To-Print Phonics* program.

---

* See appendix, page 147 for instructions for making a listening post (Junction Box). Approximate cost is provided.

** Durrell, Donald D. and Helen A. Murphy, *Durrell-Murphy Phonics Practice Program,* Self-directing, Self-correcting Phonics Picture Cards, New York: Harcourt Brace Jovanovich, Inc., 1968.

It is important that all children recognize letters by name, both capital and lowercase, early in the reading program. Most letter names contain their sounds, and this assists the child in relating the phoneme in the spoken word to its form in print. . . . The average child knows the names of twelve capital letters and nine lowercase letters when he enters school.

In their program, they "introduce the twenty-six letters of the alphabet in words commonly seen by children" (5). These words, ones that children must know in the school setting, are *look, stop, exit, fire, boys, girls, danger, school zone, quiet, jobs*, milk,* and *visitors.***

To get ready for this activity and to develop interest in it, the children can be taken for a walk through and around the school. The teacher will stop the group at the location where one of the above words is found and talk about it. Most of the words can be found on this tour.

Manuscript, Word Study, and Writing Combined

After this tour, the teacher should introduce the words one or two at a time, first with capital letters, then using lowercase. The words can be placed on ditto sheets so that the child can practice writing them with proper manuscript. Since so many of these words lend themselves to writing activities, the advanced child can use them in writing simple sentences. Finally, each of the words can be written by the children on individual cards to be placed in their word collection boxes.

Daily Word Study Period

After the children have been introduced to all of the letters of the alphabet in a meaningful way, it is time for the teacher to have a definite period every day for phoneme development. One of the conclusions in the analysis of the *Cooperative Research Program in First-Grade Reading Instructions* by Drs. Guy Bond and Robert Dykstra was "Word study skills must be emphasized and taught systematically regardless of what approach to initial reading instruction is used" (2).

It is very important that word study is not done during the process of decoding a book. It is done at an entirely separate time when children are grouped *by the teacher* according to their needs for mastering certain

---

* Experienced classroom teachers will think of many duties to list under "jobs." The writer would like to suggest to the inexperienced teacher that the job of sharpening pencils is one to assign on a rotating basis. Allowing children to sharpen pencils—at will—during the day can create a problem in room control.

** Durrell, Donald D. and Helen A. Murphy, *Speech-to-Print Phonics, Teacher's Manual,* New York: Harcourt Brace Jovanovich, Inc., 1964, p. 143. Used by permission.

phonic generalizations revealed through their reading and writing. Drs. Durrell and Murphy have pointed out that "about one-third of all children entering first grade are unable to identify phonemes in spoken words, while the others have the ability in differing degrees. This weakness is the most common cause of reading failure" (5). This does not mean that these children have hearing problems that affect normal oral communication, but that they have difficulty in isolating and discriminating phonemes within words.

For both reading and writing, children must first master consonant sounds in initial, terminal, and medial positions. Beginning reading can be successful with knowledge of consonant sounds *only.* Children's creative writing also can be performed with knowledge and use of consonant sounds only, if teachers initially are willing to accept misspelled words. Spelling mastery comes later and requires a study of vowel sounds and their graphic representation.

Dr. Roach Van Allen has emphasized "there is a closer relationship between phonics and writing than between phonics and reading" (1). Writing causes the child to learn phonics inductively as he has to think of the symbols to represent the sound he wants to write. Drs. Bond and Dykstra substantiate this position.

> A writing component is likely to be an effective addition to a primary reading program. In the first place, the Language Experience approach, which involves considerable written expression, was an effective program of instruction. In addition, programs such as i.t.a. and Phonic/Linguistic . . . encourage pupils to write symbols as they learn to recognize them and to associate them with sounds. This appears helpful to the pupil in learning sound-symbol relationships. Furthermore, it is likely that writing such common, but irregular, words as "the" (come, done, etc.) helps the child to commit them to his sight vocabulary (2).

For this kind of word study teaching, the teacher must keep individual record cards of each child. As suggested before, 5 x 8 inch cards are the best kind to use in the reading circle. It is particularly important that any of the Dolch* basic words, missed by the child as he reads, be

---

* Dolch, E. W., *Teaching Primary Reading* (Champaign, Illinois: The Garrard Press, 1941). The Dolch basic sight vocabulary of 220 service words makes up about sixty-five percent of all the words in the reading material of the primary grades. A listing of these words can be found in most reading text books.

The Barbe Reading Skills Check List (Readiness level through sixth grade) includes Dolch words as well as a listing of other word analysis skills needed for developing independent readers: Barbe, Walter B., *BARBE READING SKILLS CHECK LIST,* 3124 Cuyahoga Falls, Ohio, 1960., 5¢ per sheet. Every teacher should have a copy as a guide for developing necessary word study skills.

noted. The record of all words missed should be transferred to a reading skills checklist—kept in each child's personal classroom file—to aid in evaluating specific skill development needed for diagnostic teaching.

Grouping children for word study becomes a simple process when cards are used in the reading circle for keeping a record of words children need while reading orally to the teacher. The cards from all three teams can be sorted, putting together the cards indicating the particular skills needed by certain groups of children. These groups will no doubt be very flexible as some of the children will develop a generalization about a skill much faster than others. This is likely the only time that homogeneous grouping will become necessary in the classroom; slow maturing children need more time for development of specific phoneme-grapheme relationships. When presenting to children the plan about personal choices in grouping, it must be pointed out that this process operates two ways—the teacher also has "the right" to group. If it is only done for one or two purposes, it will not damage the child's self-concept.

SPEED OF DEVELOPMENT OF THESE PROJECTS

How fast a teacher incorporates and develops reading, manuscript, and word study activities into the classroom will depend upon the maturity of the children involved. Some children may not be ready to form reading teams on the second day of school as suggested. This beginning step in signing up for activities may not take place until the second week of school.

It should be remembered that reading is never defined narrowly; picture reading is acceptable if that is what the child can read. Likewise, talking about pictures, discussing sequence, and giving an individual interpretation of pictures are important to language development upon which later success in reading is based. *But the child should be free to choose the group in which he does it!* The teacher, however, should assume responsibility for guiding the child to choose a reading book at his instructional level. This can be done in the individual reading conferences. It must be kept in mind that a child cannot succeed in reading if he is missing more than one word in twenty.*

This chapter was specifically written to point out how a beginning or experienced first-grade teacher could move into teaching that protects the self-concept of the child. It is also hoped to help teachers in upper

---

* See appendix, page 149, for information on testing with an Informal Reading Inventory to determine the child's independent and instructional level of reading.

grades. After employing these techniques, first-grade teacher Mary Ellen Wollenberg said,

I want to start at the beginning of the year what I finally started in April. I realize now the importance of mobility of children; I realize the harm I did to children by keeping them in rigid groups. There was not enough time, starting in April, to overcome the damage that I know I did, and to one little girl in particular. The tone for the whole year's teaching is set on the first day of school. I know what I did in teaching phonics was correct, because the children were able to be so independent in their writing when we "unstructured" ourselves. I know that keeping them in the rigid groups for other activities was wrong and I shall never do it again. While some may think grouping is good for the children, I feel now that it has been set up only to help the teacher, to make it easier for her to plan. It was not set up thinking of what happens to children.

The first day of school is where it starts. Teachers must use their knowledge in imaginative ways to make all children feel good about themselves so they will want to learn. This does not mean the neglect of teaching basic skills which produce independent readers and writers. Initially, this is a difficult task. Later it will give way to freedom for both the teacher and the children. This occurs when children are turned loose to solve problems!

REFERENCES

1. Allen, Roach Van, and Halvorsen, Gladys C. *The Language-Experience Approach to Reading Instruction.* New York: Ginn and Co., 1961.

2. Bond, Guy L., and Dykstra, Robert. *Reading Research Quarterly.* Newark, Delaware: International Reading Association, 1967, p. 122, No. 1, p. 124, No. 3.

3. Brogan, Peggy, and Fox, Lorene K. *Helping Children Read.* New York: Holt, Rinehart and Winston, Inc., 1961.

4. Durr, William K., ed. *Reading Instruction Dimensions and Issues.* Boston: Houghton-Mifflin Co., 1967, pp. 101-102.

5. Durrell, Donald D., and Murphy, Helen A. *Speech-To-Print Phonics.* New York: Harcourt, Brace Jovanovich, Inc., 1964.

6. Humphry, James H., and Moore, Virginia D. *Games and Stunts to Read and Play,* illustrated by Ted Schroeder. Champaign, Illinois: Garrard Publishing Co., 1962, Set 1 and 2.

7. Martin, Bill, Jr. *Sounds of Language Readers.* New York: Holt, Rinehart, and Winston, 1968.

8. Moffett, James. *A Student-Centered Language Arts Curriculum, Grades K-6: A Handbook for Teacher.* Boston: Houghton-Mifflin Co., 1968, p. 56.

9. Ogg, Oscar. *The 26 Letters.* New York: Thomas Y. Crowell Co., 1961.

CHAPTER THREE

Nongraded Teaching in a Self-Contained Classroom

Up through the sixties, much was written and discussed in the name of "nongrading."

In 1963, Jerome Bruner* said:

> The nongraded system forces a complete re-evaluation of what one is trying to accomplish in the educational enterprise. . . . Nongrading comes to terms with the obvious fact of variability [in the classroom]. Some students can go faster than their age-mates, phenomenally faster, whether because of capacity [maturation], or the fortune of background. If one demands a standard amount of work from all in any given grade, may we not be robbing the student of learning and using his own pace? (3)

For the most part, administratively, it has been felt that "variability" among children could best be handled by homogeneous grouping, either within the room or between rooms. The kind of school organization described in Chapter One usually results. In addition, the feeling has been widespread that a teacher can perform more efficiently with children as the range in reading ability is decreased (4). This thinking places children in groups related to their scores received on a standardized achievement test. Advocates of this type of organization tend to

---

* Professor of Psychology and Director of the Center for Cognitive Studies, Harvard University.

Jerome Bruner, Preface to *The Appropriate Placement School: A Sophisticated Nongraded Curriculum* by Frank Brown. Englewood Cliffs, New Jersey: Prentice-Hall, Inc., 1965. Permission to quote granted by publisher.

place emphasis upon the assumption that all children learn skills in a prescribed sequence.

NONGRADING FOR THE SEVENTIES

John Goodlad and Robert Anderson, in their revised edition of *The Nongraded Elementary School*, point out that:

> The nongraded school is designed to implement a theory of continuous pupil progress: since the differences among children are great and since these differences cannot be substantially modified, school structure must facilitate the continuous educational progress of each pupil. Some pupils, therefore, will require a longer period of time than others for achieving certain learnings and attaining certain developmental levels. This theory of continuous progress differs markedly from two other prevailing theories of pupil progress: the theory of grade standards and the theory of "social" promotion. . . . To remove grades without first understanding and accepting this theory of continuous pupil progress is to court local disaster and to discredit the nongraded school movement.

They go on to say:

> There is nothing in nongrading that necessitates or even suggests any specific pattern of interclass grouping. *Nongrading** is designed to encompass the stark realities of individual differences . . . *in no way is it intended to reduce the range of individual differences with which teachers must cope.* . . . Learning now becomes a longitudinal or developmental process, each child proceeding irregularly, but never according to the prearranged stop-and-go of grade barriers. Each learner achieves his own unique insights as he proceeds (5).

A current trend to meet the nongraded philosophy is the concept of the open classroom. School construction and organization houses children, several teachers, and paraprofessionals in one large area in place of separate classrooms: e.g., early elementary children would be in one large area; upper elementary in another. Within this open classroom setting prescriptive teaching is carried on by tracking children according to needed skill development in each subject area. A child's skill achieve-

---

* Emphasis this author's.

ment might place him in one track for reading and another for mathematics.

Another organizational framework based upon the continuous pupil progress theory is the unit-experience approach in a self-contained classroom.

UNIT-EXPERIENCE APPROACH IN A
SELF-CONTAINED CLASSROOM

The unit-experience approach to learning must be accompanied by diagnostic reading skill development in a laboratory setting. This makes nongraded teaching in a self-contained classroom possible. Children of varying achievement levels are kept together, who otherwise share only similar age. Communication skills (discussion, writing, reading) are developed in relevant thematic teaching units through interchange of ideas as a topic is explored. Children are motivated to select an area of study within the framework of social studies or science in which they become personally involved. Such involvement leads to inquiry and understanding and a learning atmosphere prevails, fostering individuality. Democratic values also are developed as children are encouraged to help each other while working in a heterogeneous group. There are no red marks for failure and no stars for excellence. Skills are learned as teachers support children in positive ways keeping in mind, "I criticize by creation."* The skill of reading is not viewed simply as a decoding process but as one that is acquired as an outgrowth of using language in meaningful ways where each skill interacts with another. This is the kind of pacing that succeeds. This is the essence of "continuous pupil progress."

The unit-experience approach to learning contrasts sharply with the unrelated separate organization of subject matter, e.g., short periods of prescribed teaching of reading, spelling, science, social studies. With subject matter isolated, learning can be impeded. Concern with time schedules for each of these isolated subjects can interfere with the child's needs for time to explore, discover, and relate learnings. Children

---

* Quotation from Cicero. Teachers "criticize by creation" as they help children learn inductively by, e.g., placing the correct spelling of words above children's misspelled words, *not* red circling them; typing children's stories in correct form for the group storybook; making tapes of grade level reading material so that children of different achievement levels can have access to the same facts for class discussion.

need to feel that "our time is the time needed to explore and discover" (1). Admittedly, this is at first a more difficult kind of classroom organization. But once in operation its advantages will compensate for the initial planning and effort. With this open approach to classroom organization, it will soon be discovered that the room becomes a learning laboratory.

DISCUSSION OF TECHNIQUES

The remainder of this chapter will supplement the discussion begun in Chapter Two regarding methodology needed for meeting individual differences in a self-contained classroom. The techniques for this method are many among which the following are critical and are now discussed in detail:

Choral Reading
Group Storybook Writing
Informal Word Study
Individualized Reading and Research

STARTING EACH DAY WITH CHORAL READING

In the classroom where emphasis is placed upon language development, what happens at the beginning of the day sets the learning atmosphere for the rest of the day. Introducing units of study with related poetry, chorally read, personally extends each child's grasp of language *regardless of his reading ability.* Choral reading of poetry involves children naturally in the following activities:

1. Working together as a unified group
2. Committing to memory simple poems that can be used for choral speaking
3. Developing critical and interpretive thinking by reacting to ideas in poetry
4. Developing language abilities and vocabulary through sentence expansion, accompanied by selection and discussion of interesting words
5. Introducing informal word study
6. Promoting ideas for independent writing
7. Motivating selection of unit topic to be studied

Procedures the Teacher Must Use to Conduct
Successful Choral Reading

1. Poetry must be read with expression and enthusiasm. It takes practice ahead of class presentation to develop these qualities in the voice in order to command the attention of all children.

2. Seating should be arranged so that the teacher is eye level, or nearly so, with the children. This is accomplished by either having the children sit on the floor with the teacher sitting on a small chair or by all sitting on children's chairs.

3. Open-end questions should be carefully prepared to provoke pupil interaction as well as critical thinking. Questions relating to definition of words, semantics, synonyms, antonyms, and homonyms should be included for vocabulary development.

4. Children should be taught to use markers: the child with visual and word recognition problems is enabled to keep his place; the fast achieving child is held to the correct pace of the poem.

5. To insure success for the slow achieving child in the group choral reading situation, *advanced* introduction to the new poetry should take place. This can be done via tape in the listening center or in the pupil-teacher conference in the reading circle. (see p. 20)

Children love to sing. Singing appropriate songs daily, as an introduction to choral reading, reinforces the idea that there are no "solo" parts in poetry read chorally and reminds the faster reader not to rush ahead. With each child having a copy of the poem being read, children are assisted in relating the sounds of the words to the symbol. For this reason, the poems used should be printed or typed so that sufficient individual copies are available. Children should be taught to place their poem collections in inexpensive three-hole folders so that they will develop a personalized poetry book for daily use.

In this opening exercise of choral reading, it is good to include short selections of simple poetry which soon are committed to memory and can be used for *choral speaking* as the appropriate time arises throughout the day, e.g., lining up to go to the lunchroom or playground. Instead of punching and pushing each other as they wait in line, children are caught up in the rhythm of the poetry. *Choral speaking* also can be used simply for relaxation. Selections from Mother Goose such as "One Misty Moisty Morning," "The North Wind Doth Blow," "The Old Cow Died with a Bug in Her Ear" are good for this purpose, as well as, "White Sheep, White Sheep" ("Clouds").

Keep a Poem in Your Pocket

Keep a poem in your pocket
and a picture in your head
and you'll never feel lonely
at night when you're in bed.

The little poem will sing to you
the little picture bring to you
a dozen dreams to dance to you
at night when you're in bed.

Beatrice Schenk de Regniers

The Clouds

White sheep, white sheep,
    On a blue hill,
When the wind stops,
    You all stand still.

You walk far away,
    When the winds blow;
White sheep, white sheep,
    Where do you go?

Folder decorated by child

"Clouds" is particularly well suited to inspire independent writing later in the day. The stories on pages 33-36, written and illustrated by first-grade children, demonstrate this.

The following story on "Clouds" was written after the teacher involved the class in sentence expansion, developed from their kernel sentence, "Clouds float."

The Clouds

The clouds are white and fluffy. When the wind blows the clouds float for miles and miles. When the wind doesn't blow the clouds stand still.

If you look outside you can see different shapes, like a rabbit or shoe or a man or a bed or a clock and other shapes.

These are only some of the shapes I saw on my trip around the school.

Joseph C., second grade

Suggestion: A science unit on cloud formation can evolve from this introduction.

"Keep a Poem in Your Pocket," from *Something Special*, © 1958, by Beatrice Schenk de Regniers. Reprinted by permission of Harcourt Brace Jovanovich, Inc.

Unknown, "White Sheep, White Sheep," from *The Arbuthnot Anthology of Children's Literature—Time for Poetry*, compiled by May Hill Arbuthnot. Glenview, Illinois: Scott Foresman and Company, 1961, p. 156.

How Clouds Work

The clouds are on a blue hill.
The thunder booms like a cannon.

The clouds are blue.
The clouds look like animals.

The clouds are stiff when the wind stops.

Sometimes the clouds have vanished like a witch. that is sad.

Sheep, White
Sheep, White
Where aie you

I am at
The Ann-
amal. Zoo

white

This dog
is a
big cloud

After chorally reading a selection together, the teacher should ask the children if anyone heard a word he enjoyed saying or a new word he did not understand. As the children respond, the words are printed upon cards for the child to claim and file in his "word box" or copy in his own "dictionary" for use later in writing stories.

Children should be encouraged to use word substitution in combination with choral reading. This is particularly successful when simple nonsense poems are used, such as:

> Listen, listen and you shall hear,
> How the old cow died with a bug in her ear.
> The bug flew out,
> The wind blew in,
> And the old cow's up and gone again.*

It makes no difference whether the reader is a slow achiever or a fast achiever, the use of oral language will take over as his imagination is turned loose in substituting words for "cow," "bug," or any other words which come to mind. Such oral-language fun can later be expanded to drawing pictures, illustrating each new version of the poems, and writing stories about them.

A poem made up of kernel sentences, such as the following, can be used effectively to develop interest in a nature theme, which for the more mature children may develop into a study of ecology.

> Jump or Jiggle
>
> Frogs jump.
> Caterpillars hump.
> Worms wiggle.
> Bugs jiggle.
> Rabbits hop.
> Horses clop.
> Snakes slide.
> Sea gulls glide.
> Mice creep.
> Deer leap.
> Puppies bounce.
> Kittens pounce.

---

* From the book *The American Mother Goose,* by Ray Wood, Copyright, 1940 by Ray Wood. Copyright renewed, © 1968, by Willis J. Wood. Reprinted by permission of J. B. Lippincott Company.

Lions stalk.
But
I walk.*

Evelyn Beyer

Surprisingly enough, this poem appeals to all children in the primary grades when presented properly. What one does with it later will depend upon the maturity of the children. For example, activities in kindergarten and the first grade might be related simply to acting out the movements suggested, classifying animals and insects, and deciding which one would make the best pet. Follow-through activities would include going on short, informal field trips to find worms or bugs, making likenesses of the living beings mentioned in the poem at the make-it table, writing (dictating), and reading stories about them. More mature primary children can be stimulated from this poem to do a scientific study leading to deeper understanding of ecology.

Regardless of the age level, this poem lends itself well to language development through sentence expansion (see page 57 for detailed instructions on sentence expansion). Moreover, choral reading should be followed by such an activity with the whole class participating. As individual responses are written on the chalkboard, the way to write interesting sentences is demonstrated. Such a demonstration helps the child to write his own story, choosing the sentence he likes best as a starter. The teacher should also recognize the opportunity presented by this simple poem, as well as the others, for informal word study. Leading the child to underline initial and ending consonants and consonant blends will aid in the child's development of these sounds which are reinforced later in his storywriting.

The following is an expressive windy-day poem which can be used in a study unit on weather. In addition, children are motivated to write when they learn that it was written by a nine-year-old child. They become anxious to read it and later try writing their own poems, and they should be encouraged to sign their individual attempts with their own names and ages—thus encouraging development of a positive self-concept.

The Wind

The wind!
Whooshing, swishing,

Howling, pushing,
That's the wind!
The wind is cold.
The wind is chilly.
Wind!
Screeching, sneezing,
Breezing, freezing,
That's the wind!
Dash!
Tumble weeds roll,
Trash cans crash,
Smash!
The dirt flies high,
Dust gets in your eye,
That's the wind!*

William (age 9)

An informal word study can initiate from "The Wind." For example, a good beginning is to discuss the /ng/ word endings. After children are asked what letters represent this /ng/** they are told to find the number of /ngs/ in the poem. This search becomes a game for the children as they make their analysis. Next they are led to distinguish the difference between /w/ and the digraph /wh/ by placing their hands in front of their mouths to see what happens when they pronounce "wind" and then "whooshing" and "wheezing." Immediately they discover that they feel air on their hand when pronouncing the latter two words starting with "wh" as contrasted to none when they pronounce "wind." Development of auditory and visual discrimination of many consonant blends can follow. This poem is also good for discussion of contractions.***

In summary, choral reading provides:

1. An enjoyable means for putting language patterns into children's
   ears

---

* Allen, Roach Van and Claryce Allen, *Language Experiences in Reading, Teacher's Resource Book,* Level II, Unit 3, p. 154. Encyclopaedia Britannica Press, Chicago, Illinois, 1966. Used with permission.

** *It is preferable* for volunteers to write the graphemes *i n g* on the chalkboard instead of naming them.

*** This and like poems are good to put on tape for the child to use in the listening center. A child slow in developing auditory-visual discrimination of consonant blends, digraphs, and inflectional endings should be instructed to underline certain specifics while listening to the poem. The poem with the underlined parts should be readily available to the child for checking correct answers.

2. Motivation for further language development, e.g., sentence expansion, creative writing

3. A common language experience for introducing a unit

4. A discussion base for giving direction to a unit

5. Interesting material for informal word study

GROUP STORYBOOK WRITING

The child who is not ready to read (decode) can be helped to understand that "reading is talk written down" (2). From his experiences relating to the unit of study, gained from choral reading, picture books, audiovisual viewing, field trips, etc., he will make his contribution through discussion and dictation as he observes and explores. *The child who is ready to read* will likewise participate in all of the above activities supplemented with independent reading. He will be able to write his own stories and/or reports with little help from the teacher. The contributions of all the children can be made into student books to be read by all.

Combining the reports or stories of children of differing levels of maturity into a common class-made book has proven to be a very successful activity to help all children feel that they "belong" to and are capable of being active participants in their group. It makes no difference that one or two of the stories in the booklet have been dictated to the teacher while others have been written independently. The difference disappears when put in booklet form as illustrated by the following examples on pages 41 and 42 of booklets written by groups of first and second graders on the theme of nature and wildlife.

A unit on spring, in which the scarecrow played an important part in the discussion, prompted four children in a first-grade i.t.a.* room to write the following storybook on pages 43 and 44.

The children's original stories, whether written out by the child or dictated, are edited by the teacher and placed in correct form in the group booklet. This provides inductive teaching of spelling and sentence structure as the child sees his story in correct form. The children then follow through with the project by illustrating and making appropriate individualized covers for their books. The finished books are placed on the reading table along with other books and can be selected for indi-

---

* i.t.a. (Initial Teaching Alphabet) is basically a phonemic approach to beginning reading. The program uses forty-four symbols, each of which represents one sound. Its symbols are in lowercase letters only.

Nature
and
Wildlife

WILDLIFE OF DEER

Deer are very beautiful. Their only protection is their beautiful camouflage and their great speed.
A fawn is brown and on the back, black with white spots. A doe is brown with a white tail. A buck is brown and the only deer with horns. Hunting season is in autumn --- and that is the end.

— Joel W.

FROGS

Frogs are slimy and green with black spots. They swim with their hind feet. Sometimes they jump about twenty feet and some are five inches long

— Greg K.

THE RABBIT

Rabbits are very cuddly. Rabbits are brown, black, grey, and white. They live in cages, holes, and woods. They have long ears and short puffy tails.

Rabbit season is in the fall. Some people like to eat rabbits, but some people like to have them for pets. I would like them for a pet.

– Jill C.

THE SNAKE

One kind of snake is poisonous. They crawl in the grass and the only shelter they have is grass. You wouldn't want to meet up with one, though. They mostly live in the jungle. They are mostly green.

– David H.

THE FUNNY BEAR

Once upon a time there was a bear. This bear was not the kind you see in the woods because he was a funny bear. One day a hunter came into the woods with his gun. He was hunting for a bear. When the bear saw the hunter he went up the tree, so the man went back to the car. When he was going to the car, the bear jumped down on his back and he went to the car with the man. When he got home his wife took her pan and spanked the bear and the bear lived happily ever after, but the man and his wife didn't.

– Tracey S.

spring

tabl ov contents

m ie scærcroe

spring

m ie scærcroe

a scaercroe can scaer
yω out ov yωr wits
and you miet forget Jhat
yω maed it.
   doen't forget that
yω maed it.

                    —James R.

m ie scærcroe

ie liek mie scærcroe.
hee dusn't hav eny braens.
soe hee is dum and funny.
   hee is floppy becaus
hee is stufft.
   hee scaers croes awæ
very well.

                    —Eddie S.

mie scaercroe

a scaercroe scaers croes. ie hav a scaercroe. When ie hav noe frends ie plae with him. it is mor and mor fun.

— Valerie R.

sprirg

in sprirg, aull the girls and bois brirg out thaer bieks and ried them.

the birds sirg and thae maek thaer nests.

— Billy P.

vidual oral reading to the teacher in the reading circle. Imagine what motivation this provides, particularly for the slower child when he sees his name as the author of an interesting story, written correctly, in the same book with those of the fast achievers. It is true he may be able to

Once upan a time there Wheis a lettle man that loved fish and everyday He ate fish

you wouldn't no how many He ate once a

day

Child's story before editing

read only the story he wrote, but it will act as a positive incentive for him to work harder at word study to acquire additional writing and reading skills.

Children reading their own books in the reading circle

INFORMAL WORD STUDY

As mentioned previously, opportunities for informal word study arise when poems are chorally read. Such study should never be overdone since the enjoyment of the melody of the poetry is the primary goal of choral reading. However, skillful use of the suggested techniques already discussed, can be very beneficial to all children and enable the slower reader to participate in a meaningful way. They also will reinforce the formal diagnostic word study program of the room.

Another informal word study class activity can be developed through sentence games using only consonants and context: Th– br––n r–bb–t r–ns f–st.*

Teachers who have used this technique successfully have placed some meaningful sentence on the chalkboard before the children arrive, such as: "G––d m–rn–ng ch–ldr–n, l–t's pl–n a f––ld tr–p f–r th–s –ft–rn––n"; or "F–ve ch–ldr–n c–n s–gn –p f–r w–rk –t th– m–k– –t t–bl– fr–m 9:30 t– 10:00." Children really enjoy figuring out these

---

* The Old Testament of the Bible was written with only consonants in its first version. Since knowledge of vowels came later, no space was left for vowels.

coded messages. In order to allow the slower reader more time to figure them out, the teacher requests each one to keep it a secret until a certain specified time when he has the whole class read them together.

The consonant-context plan can have three purposes: 1) to test the children's knowledge of consonant sounds in beginning, medial, and terminal positions, 2) to encourage better use of context in reading, and 3) to make the children freer in expressing themselves in writing.

Children who have not had the opportunity to "grow" into reading seem apprehensive to express themselves in writing; usually they are too fearful of misspelling a word. Playing the consonant-context game is a good way to overcome this fear.

Along with repeated use of poetry, the consonant-context game proved to be a very successful way of motivating two boys in particular to begin using language beautifully. A second-grade teacher* in pre-service training had had no success in getting these two second-grade boys to develop in creative writing. One especially was obsessed with talking and writing about monsters. A unit on wildlife proved to be a splendid one to redirect this enthusiasm in a positive way. The teacher checked out books from the library on wild and tame animals and encouraged the boys to find other books on this subject. The children began to categorize living and extinct animals, leading to much discussion. No longer did monsters come into the conversation! Their teacher, however, still could not get them to write.

After finding out how fascinated the boys were with his presentation of sentences leaving out the vowels, he was able to get them to use this game method to write for him. He then showed them some of the prewritten sentences which he had taken from poetry. After doing this

---

* Robert Kemppainen, 1970 graduate, Northern Michigan University.

for a while, he showed them a book entitled *Poems for Weather Watching*.* Here is what he wrote in his evaluation:

> I used the book, *Poems for Weather Watching*, and had the boys draw pictures and write stories about the different kinds of weather and the activities which could be carried out in these kinds of weather. After we read each of the poems together, I had the children write in the little booklets I had prepared for them ahead of time. The boys continued to write—the whole period. They would have continued longer if the bell had not rung ending the period! (See stories on page 48)

INDIVIDUALIZED READING AND RESEARCH

Once a unit theme is established the teacher collects suitable and appropriate reading material. The reading center should include basal readers; subject texts; library, picture, trade and reference books—in numbers and variety sufficient to span individual reading levels and interests found within the group. The children are then encouraged to browse through the collection of books and choose ones to read for pleasure or to gain information on the unit.

A team is called to the reading circle, each child with his chosen book. In individualized reading, the child takes a turn sitting beside the teacher and reads a short passage orally for diagnostic purposes. The teacher is prepared with individual cards to note, inconspicuously, omissions, insertions, unknown words, mispronunciations, trouble with inflectional variants, and intonation.** The rest of the children in the group read independently until their turn comes to read orally to the teacher.*** As the child reads a passage orally during the pupil-teacher

---

* Isrnel, Laurie, *Poems for Weather Watching*, illustrated by Gilbert Riswald, New York: Holt, Rinehart and Winston, Inc., 1963.

** At the end of each day the teacher evaluates the reading errors noted on the anecdotal cards. Children with similar problems are grouped for specific skill development: e.g., recognition of initial and ending consonant phoneme-grapheme relationships (single, blends, and digraphs), inflectional variants, compound words. Basal stories dealing with these specific skills can be used for practice. Children working in pairs or small groups can *chorally* read the selected passage after underlining the graphemes representing the phonemes or inflectional variants being studied. In addition, tapes (preferably teacher prepared) can be used to accompany the study of specific word study skills in the listening center. Aural reinforcement is a most important ingredient in learning phoneme-grapheme relationships.

*** Another variation for organizing individualized reading, which the writer has found to be much enjoyed by first graders and which is different from the reading circle, is for each child, with his selected book, to sit on the floor in "train formation." Each one, in turn, takes a chair beside the teacher for oral reading, then returns to his own desk either to continue reading independently or do assigned seatwork.

Chuck's Story

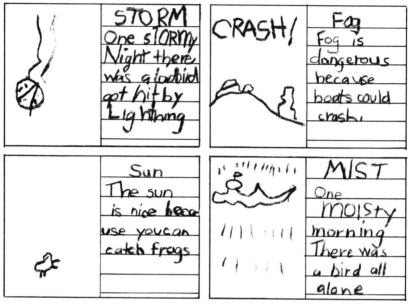

Bob's Story

conference, the teacher learns whether his selection is proper for successful reading. If more than one word in twenty is missed as he reads, the teacher should join in with the child and read it chorally with him. The child should later be helped to find a book appropriate for his reading level. For comprehension checking, *both* literal and open-ended questions should be used, as well as inquiry about meaning of unusual words within the reading context.

This type of reading is very different from that done in most teacher-directed reading groups where each child in the circle has the same book and "round-robin" reading is the usual procedure. In the "round-robin" circle every child is told to keep their eyes on the same paragraph following along with the oral reader who may struggle to pronounce words.

Oral Reading

Since it takes time to develop techniques, it is necessary for one ultimatum to be issued. *Never* allow the better reader to read orally in front of the slow-achieving child unless it is in an audience situation where no one else has a book. Differences in children's reading ability are not necessarily related to I.Q. but are related to slow growth patterns, perceptual problems, or lack of success on the part of the school in finding out how a particular child learns. With this definitely in mind, it must be stressed that nothing must be done to make the slower-achieving child feel more insecure than he already does. Thus, oral reading heard by the children either should be done by the teacher, by a child in an audience situation, or by the children *in unison.* When the child reads orally, he must do so privately *to the* teacher. *Oral reading to the teacher only* is important for diagnostic teaching. Opportunity for private oral reading must be provided *daily* in the primary grades to all children whose independent achievement level of reading is less than high second grade.

Outlining, a Prerequisite for Research

The process of outlining when taught as an isolated skill is meaningless but becomes relevant when applied to planning a party, a project, a field trip, etc. On such occasions the teacher should demonstrate to the class how ideas are organized into outline form. Outlines may be made in topical form or in sentence form as long as consistency is maintained. The sentence form is easier for the younger child to follow and develop.

Major principles for a teacher to remember in *demonstrating the development of the outline are*:

1. The outline should have an introductory and a concluding topic or sentence.
2. Each major topic should be of comparable importance and directly related to the subject of the outline.
3. There must be at least two subtopics under each major topic.
4. The same form for numbering, lettering, indenting, capitalizing, and punctuation should be used throughout the outline.
5. There should be no punctuation after the topics unless they are complete sentences (6).

While the teacher always demonstrates the correct form, the main concern in the primary grades is that the children are able to organize their ideas in *sequential order* as to relative importance. The form of the outline is secondary at this point. Emphasis upon form should be delayed until the middle grades.

In pursuing a unit study there will be many opportunities for making outlines. The teacher should get the children in the habit of using the five Ws—Who, What, When, Why, Where—in posing questions for inquiry and problem solving. Questions should be organized as to priority and importance in outline form. Then the task of finding the answers from books, encyclopedias, members of the community, and other sources becomes an orderly process. Researching for specific information helps to prevent copying from books. The primary grades are not too soon to help children *report* what they read *in their own words*. Otherwise, plagiarism may be well established by the middle grades!

Introductory skills in outlining begin in kindergarten when children are led to classify articles of any kind. Such activities lay the groundwork for clear thinking which is the basis for outlining. For example, children are told to name all of the fruits or vegetables they know. The teacher lists the responses on the chalkboard, categorizing them under the two headings. Children can be shown how to develop a simple outline from this classification by relating the fruits and vegetables to locations where they are grown. For kindergarteners, this outline may consist of only two major topics: I. These fruits grow in our neighborhood, II. These fruits do not grow in our neighborhood. For older children, a social studies unit can be developed from an outline set up as follows:

I. These fruits and vegetables grow in our neighborhood.
A.
B.
Etc.

II. These fruits and vegetables grow in the South.

A.

B.

Etc.

III. These fruits and vegetables grow in the North.

A.

B.

Etc.

From the simple start of listing fruits and vegetables that children name and organizing them into an outline, the groundwork is laid for a study of maps, topography, climate, soil, available water from lakes and rivers, transportation—as well as the people who live in the area.

Continuous Pupil Progress Results

Teachers will discover from using these techniques while working with children of differing abilities that motivation comes from language activities which are enjoyed by all of the children together. From these activities, the more mature children will find it easy to work on their own, independently reading, researching, and writing. Thus, more time is available for the teacher to give individual attention to the less mature children.

The culminating result is that each child will be free to seek his own individual level and rate of contribution toward a unit theme shared by all. Each experiences the satisfaction of being accepted as an equal, starting at a common learning point. Each is encouraged to take part in activity meaningful to him which develops his understanding of the unit. In this environment, no child feels he has nothing to contribute; each is an important working member of his class.

REFERENCES

1. Alcorn, Marvin D.; Kinder, James S.; and Schunert, Jim R. *Better Teaching in Secondary Schools,* third edition. New York: Holt, Rinehart and Winston, Inc., 1954.

2. Allen, Roach Van, and Halvorsen, Gladys C. *The Language-Experience Approach to Reading Instruction.* New York: Ginn and Co., 1961.

3. Brown, B. Frank. *The Appropriate Placement School: A Sophisticated Nongraded Curriculum.* West Nyack, New York: Parker Publishing Co., 1965, pp. XI and XII.

4. Brown, B. Frank. *The Appropriate Placement School: A Sophisticated Nongraded Curriculum.* West Nyack, New York: Parker Publishing Co., 1965, p. 55.

5. Goodlad, John I., and Anderson, Robert H. *The Nongraded Elementary School.* New York: Harcourt Brace Jovanovich, Inc., 1963.

6. Greene, Harry A., and Petty, Walter T. *Developing Language Skills in the Elementary Schools,* fourth edition. Boston: Allyn & Bacon, Inc., 1971.

SUPPLEMENTARY REFERENCES

Goldmark, Bernice. *Social Studies: A Method of Inquiry.* Belmont, California: Wadsworth Publishing Co., 1968.

Ogg, Oscar. *The 26 Letters.* New York: Thomas Y. Crowell, 1961.

CHAPTER FOUR

Unit Teaching
Detailed

At this point in our history, when human life is literally threatened because of man's past disregard for the interrelationship and interdependence of all living things, schools have a most important role to play. This fact has been pointed out quite forcefully by Dr. John E. Klimas, Program Director, National Science Foundation, Washington, D.C.* He feels the only hope for the future is to develop "a new generation of adults who regard the environment as something to be lived with, nurtured and conserved." His message to the elementary school teacher is, "I'm counting on teachers to help our young people grow up into environment-conscious adults. That's our only hope. . . . Man is polluting his air, poisoning his water and upsetting the balance of life on the land."

There are four basic concepts he wants teachers to instill in their students:

1. Awareness of the diversity of things in nature. To develop this understanding, children must be given an opportunity to examine their surroundings and learn to sample, identify, and classify what they see.

2. Awareness of the interrelationship of natural things. As Klimas says, "We've got to get them to understand early that in nature you simply can't disturb one thing without disturbing others."

3. Awareness of adaptation that takes place as nature adjusts to environmental conditions.

---

* Professor of Biology at Fairfield University, Fairfield, Connecticut.

53

4. Awareness of succession: "Children need to know in their bones that the only thing constant in nature is change."

The teacher must have these four basic concepts in mind as discovery lessons are developed to help children become aware of natural environment.

The equipment needed to teach ecology on field trips and in the classroom is very simple. This equipment can be made at the "make-it" table or by the child at home. Examples:

1. Use coat hangers and cheese cloth to make nets
2. Convert old wire mesh screens into insect and small animal cages
3. Convert large glass jars or containers into terrariums for the classroom study

In addition, the classroom should have ordinary household thermometers and inexpensive microscopes. Each child should have a hand magnifying glass to use on the field trip.* A detailed procedure for developing two different units in which there is correlation of language-experience and ecology follows:

1. Ecology with emphasis upon Indian culture
2. Ecology with emphasis upon seeds and trees

ECOLOGY WITH EMPHASIS UPON INDIAN CULTURE

A most appropriate poem to use for introduction is "Indian Children."**

Indian Children

Where we walk to school each day
Indian children used to play
All about our native land,
Where the shops and houses stand.

---

* Teachers wishing further practical detailed information for the development and teaching of ecology should read "Ecology," *Grade Teacher,* Vol. 86, No. 5, January 1969, pp. 93-126. Permission granted by Dr. Klimas and *Grade Teacher* Magazine for quoting and paraphrasing from their article.

** From the book *For Days and Days* by Annette Wynne. Copyright, 1932, Renewal ©, 1960 by Annette Wynne. Reprinted by permission of J. B. Lippincott Company.

And the trees were very tall,
And there were no streets at all,
Not a church and not a steeple,
Only the woods and Indian people.

Only wigwams on the ground,
And at night bears prowling round—
What a different place today
Where we live and work and play.

Annette Wynne

The children gather informally in front of the teacher, either in chairs or on the floor, to hear the poem. While there are mimeographed copies of the poem to give to each child, they are not passed out until the appropriate time. The following steps will make for successful introduction of the poem:

1. Tell the children to close their eyes while they listen to the poem being read, trying to imagine in their minds what the poem is telling them. Also they should be told to listen for interesting words they would like to discuss. (The teacher should read slowly and expressively.)

2. Let the children discuss how the poem made them feel. Such open-ended questions as the following can be used to stimulate discussion:

   a. What different kinds of noises would you have heard *then* as contrasted with *now*—during the day? during the night?

   b. What were the interesting words in the poem that you'd like to add to your word collection?

   c. Where might we find "bears prowling round" today?

   d. What other words could we use for "prowling"?

   e. What does "native land" mean? Does "native land" mean the same thing to the Indians as it does to us?

3. Read the poem again. This time have the children supply the rhyming word for every other line.

4. Pass out the copies of the poem. Tell the children to watch while you read it, then you will have them read it with you.

While this procedure may seem slow it will insure that all children understand and participate in the choral reading and enjoy the mood of the poem. The fast readers will not rush ahead; they have found the pace at which the poem is to be read by listening to the teacher. The slow readers will be familiar enough with the poem's content and rhyming ends that they will feel success in their reading. If the teacher knows there are very slow maturing youngsters in the group as well as ones with perception problems, markers must be used. To protect the self-concept of slow readers, insist that all children use the markers at first. The faster children later can discard theirs, but in the introductory stage it helps to slow them down, while showing the slow maturing children the benefit they will derive from using markers. When all are required to use them at first, no stigma will be attached to their use.

WRITING ACTIVITIES FROM THE POEM

To maintain the mood created from reading "Indian Children," a writing activity might well take place immediately after the enjoyment of the poem. The following are examples of children's stories inspired by the choral reading of this poem:

Indians

I love Indians because they are one of us.
God made them brown.

They hunt for deer. Sometimes they hunt
for bear. They peel the fur off.

I love Indians.

Indian People

The Indians were very hungry because it was
raining. They had raw fish in their wigwam
so they ate it. First they cleaned it, then
they ate it.

When it stopped raining they went hunting
for more food.

Indian Life

Indians live all over the place. Indians
live in all kinds of things. They move all
over the place.

The Indians eat corn. The Indians kill
deer to eat.

Those children needing to dictate their stories can be encouraged to draw pictures about the way the poem makes them feel while waiting their turn for the teacher's help. Advanced preparation of blank booklets to use for the art work will serve as an incentive. A card with the words INDIAN DAYS printed on it can be inserted in each blank booklet to give guidance to the child for writing a title on the front, along with his name.

Sentence expansion, mentioned before on page 38, is an aid to stimulating writing as well as showing children how to develop sentences in their personal writing. Let's see how it can work from the poem "Indian Children." The teacher poses a question such as "What word in the poem named something particularly interesting to you?" A response might be, "Bears" (noun). The next question would be, "What do bears do?" The answer most likely will be, "prowl" (verb). With this kernel sentence written on the chalkboard, the teacher elicits describing words (adjectives) from the children to place in front of "bears," then continues by asking the children to tell how, when, and where the bears might prowl. The following example might be the result of such probing by the teacher:

	furry		softly			wigwam	
The	black bears prowl	quietly around the camp	at night.
	hungry		busily				

Different children should read their favorite sentence from the board. From this activity, they are helped to see how to write a complete sentence in an interesting way. Such preparation inspires them to write their individual stories. A group storybook on bears can result, as shown by the following stories on pages 58 and 59 written by second graders.

INFORMAL FIELD TRIP FOLLOWS

The diversified activities and research that take place after the introduction of this poem are as numerous as the combined imagination of the children and the teacher. *An informal field trip around the school grounds is a must.* If the class is lucky enough to be close to a wooded area, they should include it in the itinerary. The purpose of such an informal trip is to motivate the children to find or look at something in nature that they think Indian children may have enjoyed years ago.

Organization for the Field Trip

With a class of approximately thirty children, it would seem feasible to establish approximately six teams. To establish the teams with a

BEARS

Table of Contents

THE BLACK BEAR

The black bear hybernates in a cave. He hybernates for winter.

The black bear plays on a mountain.

The black bear goes home.

by Karen S.

THE POLAR BEAR

The polar bear swims speedily in the ocean. He is very very bad when he kills fish and penguins and walrus.

He kills the fish and the cubs. He chokes and kills the snake.

by Michael P.

THE TAME BEAR

The grizzly bear prowls slowly in the woods.
My grizzly is tame. He acts like a dog-watcher. He is good! I like my tame grizzly.
My tame grizzly is a pro.

by Robert P.

THE GRIZZLY BEAR

The grizzly bear prowls slowly in the woods. The grizzly bear is very dangerous. He eats fish and meat. He even steals farmers' chickens. The grizzly bear is a blood-thirsty. bear.

by Tom B.

maximum of speed the class can count itself off, one to five. The teacher should have prepared six sheets of notebook paper ahead of time, each with a heading Team I, Team II, on through Team VI. (An alternative to this would be to use the three teams already organized, dividing each in half.) After it has been discovered which team each child is on, he should sign his name on the appropriate sheet. (The teacher can then return the sheets to a notebook for record purposes.)

In advance planning, the teacher enlists the cooperation of the class in obtaining and preparing equipment needed for field trip collections:

1. Suitable containers must be supplied for each child to house his collection as it is gathered. For safety reasons, clear plastic bottles or cardboard boxes, with holes punched in the lids, should be used in the primary grades. Each child should have a sack.

2. Nets for catching butterflies and other winged insects should be made.

3. A large glass container—to be used as a terrarium—should be prepared by each team for depositing live collections upon return from the field trip. This will allow *indoor* study to continue after the *outdoor* study is made.

A group meeting of each team should take place for the purpose of deciding what particular articles of nature are to be sought. In these meetings each person's responsibility is defined.

And *with the ground rules laid,* the class can depart for their exploration.

Short Field Trips are Possible Regardless of the Location of the School

There may be some who will ask what aspects of nature can be found on the school groups of the inner city. This question should be put to them—is it possible that there is any place today where one can't find ants, rocks, sand, dirt, butterflies, bugs, flies, even the measuring worm? Lack of a wooded area should not prevent the class from learning about the nature around them. If little is found on the field trip, perhaps even this discovery can lead to meaningful discussions about changes that have taken place in our country and the effects they have had on our lives. Perhaps the short school-yard field trip (thirty minutes) won't be very fruitful, but it should provide the incentive for individual children to look at home for additions to the team's collection, to explore books which the teacher should have assembled for the study, and to plan a trip to a museum for additional information!

Work of Teams after Field Trips

Let's look at our six established teams. What will each of them be ready to do after the initial field trip? Certainly, any of the following:

1. Start making a mural from their collection supplemented with drawings to fill in what they did not find
2. Write a story on "What I Saw"
3. Write stories, either individually or as a team, on Indian folklore as contrasted with life today
4. Do research on any aspect of life that was found, relating it to ecology

Each team member will work at his level of competence. In addition, the teacher will support all efforts in writing. Some will need to dictate while others will be strong enough in phoneme-grapheme relationship that having help in the spelling of occasional words will suffice. Teammates will help each other in research and reporting.

It should be said here that all children of a particular team will not be interested in pursuing the study of the same thing. Some may like butterflies, others rocks, some may be more interested in bugs.

ANECDOTAL REPORTS OF TEAM WORK,
OUTDOORS AND INDOORS

A team in the third grade, organized along the lines described here, brought success to a particular boy. In the classroom he was quiet, withdrawn, and very conscious of his poor achievement in reading and writing. It was on the field trip after the introduction of this unit that Mike "opened up." When he found that two very competent members of his team (girls) were afraid to catch bugs, he proudly caught them for the girls and began talking about them. His teammates started viewing him with respect for his ability to handle live insects. When they returned to the classroom, they wanted him to write a story about what he had told them so their team could share their information with the other teams. The teacher took advantage of this situation and became immediately available for dictation. It was indeed amazing what this quiet boy had learned about insects through observation on his own. His story inspired one of the more able members of his team to go to the encyclopedia to verify what Mike had written and to learn more.

Another third-grade boy (primer instructional reading level) was inspired after a field trip to write:

Moss

Anyone who wishes to go on a moss hunt should go to a moist, shady place. Mosses are often found growing on damp soil, on tree trunks, on rocks, and on logs. Mosses are also found growing in ponds and at the bottoms of streams. These tiny plants may grow so close together they make a green carpet.

Short, informal, daily field trips make children interested in learning. Over and over again you hear children say, "I like being outside. I hate sitting!"

One teacher reported a field trip as follows:

The children were enthusiastic in talking about Indians as they walked along—what *they* would have looked for, what Indian children would have used for catching live things in place of our bottles, cartons, and nets. Eddie pretended he was an Indian and started acting out the part. He said, "I can run fast and be quiet because I wear moccasins. I've got to get my bow and arrow ready."

When we returned inside, the children drew pictures on large white paper either of what they imagined they saw or the sidewalks and other actual scenery of today. Michael had seen butterflies and, since this is his hobby, went to the library table to get a book on the subject. Although only an independent reader at primer level, he began describing to his group how he catches and studies butterflies. He was able to point out in the reference book several different kinds that he had studied. Naturally this led him to dictate and illustrate a story for his team:

My Butterfly Collection

I have five butterflies. First I caught one, then I caught four more. I'm going to catch more and put them in my collection. Today I saw two more I want to catch.

Michael aroused so much interest in butterflies that I was able to encourage others to write imaginative stories by posing the question: Where would you like to fly if you were a butterfly?

ADDITIONAL POETRY RELATED TO THE UNIT, INTRODUCED DAILY*

Each day the teacher introduces more poetry for choral reading relating to the unit. From the collection of books in the room library, as well as outside sources, children can be encouraged to join the teacher in looking for appropriate poetry to add to the daily choral reading period. The following poem lends itself to real interpretive thinking, discussions, and writings:

Circles**

The white man drew a small circle in the sand
    and told the red man,
"This is what the Indian knows,"
And drawing a big circle around the small one,
"This is what the white man knows."

The Indian took the stick
And swept an immense ring around both circles;

---

* The writer has found that the following poems from *The Arbuthnot Anthology of Children's Literature,* Chicago: Scott, Foresman and Co., 1960, fit in nicely with this unit: "The Little Whistler," Frances Frost, p. 105; "Grizzly Bear," Mary Austin, p. 121; "Crows," David McCord, p. 52. Also "Twenty Froggies," George Cooper in *Favorite Poems for the Children's Hour,* edited by Josephine Bouton, New York: Platt & Munk Publishers, 1945.

**Sandburg, Carl, "Circles," from *Wind Song* by Carl Sandburg, New York: Harcourt Brace Jovanovich, 1960, p. 56. Reprinted by permission of Harcourt Brace Jovanovich, Inc.

"This is where the white man and the red man
know nothing."

Carl Sandburg

One teacher* evaluated a lesson which used this poem with second-grade children. She said:

At first the children did not understand the use of "circles" at all. We got into a deep discussion about it after reading the poem over several times. Then, the children had a "store" of ideas to contribute. When they finally understood the author's idea they went on to develop other ideas. For example, Lucy drew a small circle and said, "This is what our baby knows," and drawing a larger circle she said, "This is what my sister knows," and she continued until she had included every member of her family with her father representing the largest circle. Then she said, "This is what none of us know." It was delightful! Steven did essentially the same thing grade one, grade two, etc. All of the children decided that the red man and the white man were just as wise because each thought he knew more than the other!

The following are examples of children's writing after a discussion of the poem:

White Man and Indians

This is what I think about the Indians and the white man.

I think the white man might know more about reading, writing and talking—where they are in the world.

The Indians know more about what animals eat, and how to plant good food.

The white man has different dress than the Indians. They have different hats or headdress. But we are all human.

Circles

The small circle for the Indian means that the Indians know little about the white man and are small in number compared to them.

The larger circle for the white man may mean that the Indian is being closed in by the white man who are more in number.

The largest circle may mean how little the two people know about each other.

---

* Jean Hallstrom, 1970 graduate, Northern Michigan University.

CONSERVATION OF NATURAL RESOURCES

A social study unit can evolve from a discussion of the last two lines of "Indian Children":

> What a different place today
> Where we live and work and play!

Interest in the conservation of natural resources can be sharpened as children thoughtfully discuss the reasons for differences in our country today.

A good format to use for evoking critical thinking and responses regarding conservation is provided in *Language Experience in Reading, Teacher's Resource Book, Level II.*, p. 234.*

WILDLIFE

When our country first began there was plenty of space for wildlife. Today wildlife is being crowded out by *pollution*, *fires*, and *factories*. Wild creatures have to find *homes* and *food* in new places.

Many people are careless with *matches*. They destroy *forests* and *animals*. Sometimes *children* are careless too.

Many birds and animals are disappearing. *Buffalos*, *fish*, and *Eagles* are just about gone. There used to be *alot* of *deer*. Now there are just a few.

To save our wildlife, many new laws are being made in our country and other countries. One of the laws is that *Sewage treatment, good farming, good forest, waste treatment.*

All of us should be proud of what we are doing to help save our wildlife. It is everybody's job.

---

* Allen, Roach Van, and Claryce Allen, Chicago, Ill.: Encyclopaedia Britannica Press, 1966. Used by permission.

Responses can lead to a meaningful study of the community in which the children live as well as the country at large.*

The five Ws should be applied—Who, What, Why, When, Where— in raising questions about what has taken the place of wildlife in the community. A study outline can be developed from questions raised, following the procedures detailed in Chapter Three.

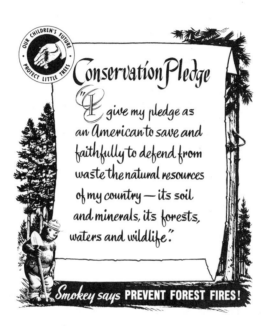

Interest in conserving natural resources in the country, aside from cities, can be heightened by children taking a Conservation Pledge. This becomes a very serious pledge as each child signs his name and discusses how he will carry it out.

ECOLOGY WITH EMPHASIS UPON SEEDS

This unit can be adapted for use any time during the year. The life cycle can be made real to children in the classroom, and its progression watched as seeds are studied and planted throughout the year. However,

---

* Since some children in the second grade will not be able to read "Wildlife" independently, the teacher should read it chorally with the children, allowing time for them to fill in their own ideas.

as described here, the unit is related only to those areas of the country that have a definite fall season.

Children love riddles; thus, the following story is most appropriate for introducing this unit to first and second graders:

The House with a Star Inside

There was once a little girl who liked riddles. She liked to ask them and she liked to guess them.

One day her mother said, "Anne, I have a riddle for you. Find the answer and bring it to me. There is a little red house near our home. It has no doors and windows. It has a star inside. The star is a bed. Five little ones are asleep in it."

"What a queer house!" said Anne. "I will ask the carpenter about it. He makes houses, I know."

So Anne ran to the carpenter. "Please, Mr. Carpenter," she said, "can you tell me where there is a little red house? It has no doors and windows. It has a star inside. The star is a bed. Five little ones are asleep in it."

The carpenter put down his saw and looked at Anne. "I never made a house like that," he said. "All the houses I build have doors and windows, and there are no stars inside."

"I will ask the postman," said Anne. "He goes along the road every day and sees all the houses near here." So Anne ran to the postman.

"Please, Mr. Postman," she said, "can you tell me where there is a little red house? It has no doors and no windows. It has a star inside. The star is a bed. Five little ones are asleep in it."

The postman put down his bag and looked at Anne. "I never saw a house like that," he said. "I carry letters to many little red houses, but they all have doors and windows, and there are no stars inside."

"I will ask the farmer," said Anne. He has many kinds of houses for his animals on the farm." So Anne ran to the farmer.

"Please, Mr. Farmer," she said, "can you tell me where there is a little red house? It has no doors and no windows. It has a star inside. The star is a bed. Five little ones are asleep in it."

The farmer was gathering apples. He stopped his work and looked at Anne. "I never saw a house like that, he said. "All the houses for my animals have doors and windows and there are no stars inside."

"Mother says there is a house like that, but I can't find it," said Anne.

"I am sorry I cannot help you find it," said the farmer, "Would you like to have one of these pretty red apples from my tree?"

"Thank you," said Anne.

She ran home with the apple in her hand. "Mother," she said, "I looked and looked for the little red house. I asked the carpenter and the postman and the farmer about it. Not one of them had ever seen a house like that."

"Oh!" said her mother.

"I could not find it," said Anne.

"What is that you have in your hand?" asked her mother.

"An apple that the farmer gave me," said Anne. "It is not a little red house with a star inside."

"Let me see," said her mother. She cut the apple through the middle. In the middle was a star. Inside the star were five little brown seeds.

"See," said Anne's mother, "the apple is the little red house. It has no doors and no windows. It has a star inside. In the star five little apple seed fairies are asleep."

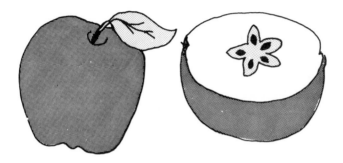

Most children have never noticed this "star with the five little apple seeds" before, and they are stimulated by it into imaginative thinking and writing. At the end of the story, in order to make this real to the children, the teacher should demonstrate by cutting an apple in half.*

A poem that is very appropriate with this unit is titled "Seeds." It should be read chorally following the same procedures for choral reading already discussed.

Seeds**

Seeds are funny, funny things
Some have stickers
Some have wings.

---

* This is a fine time to give the children a nutritious treat by having enough apples on hand to allow each child a slice to eat. To make this a quick distribution operation the teacher should have cut at least five apples ahead of time; as each apple is cut into six slices, it should be securely wrapped to insure freshness later in the classroom.

** Reprinted from *Instructor,* © October 1954, The Instructor Publications, Inc. Used by permission.

Some are big
And some are small
Some, round and flat
Some like a ball.

Some are hidden
Inside of fruits,
Some in pods
But never in roots.

Some seeds are foods
And good to eat—
Like corn and beans
Or nuts for a treat!

But whatever the kind
Or wherever it's found—
All plants grow
From a seed in the ground.

Velda Blumhagen

Since this is a long poem, with a great deal of content, it is suggested that it be made into booklet form with each of the five stanzas appearing on separate pages.

INSTRUCTIONS FOR MAKING BOOKLETS, USING THE POEM "SEEDS"

Prepare stencils with only two verses on each one—each half of the stencil will have one verse, spaced properly. Use a paper cutter to cut each mimeographed sheet in the middle so that the booklet will contain six pages, exclusive of the cover.

Covers for booklet can be made by the children from colored construction paper of their choice. To secure the pages in the booklet inside the cover, children can sew them together using darning needles *already* threaded with yarn. Booklets can be made artistic by making provision for the children to glue various seeds on the covers.

ACTIVITIES STIMULATED FROM SUCH A BOOKLET

1. After reading the poem chorally, discussions can be stimulated by open-ended questions such as:

a. How does the wind help to plant seeds?
b. How do leaves help to plant seeds?
c. What conditions must exist for seeds to grow?
d. Which seeds in the poem roll, fly, must be planted in the ground? Can you think of other seeds to add to those listed in the poem?

2. Children can use the blank sheet beside each stanza for individual illustrations and writing (dictating).

3. Informal field trips—organized as already described—can take place in search of seeds. Such trips should stimulate collections of seeds at home to be brought to school.

4. Art projects can be carried on, such as painting seeds or gluing them in interesting forms on art paper.

5. Seeds can be planted from grapefruits and oranges in the classroom. With proper care waxy green shoots will make their appearance, and the children can watch the gradual growth of their little trees throughout the school year.

6. Two acorns can be put in a quart mason jar with a paper towel between them. By keeping them watered, the children can watch them sprout and begin to grow. The purpose of the paper towel is to hold moisture, keep the acorns apart and next to the sides of the jar so they can be seen more readily.

UNIT ON SEEDS LEADS TO STUDY OF TREES

As children explore the outdoors for the seeds mentioned in the poem, they will be collecting leaves also. If it is fall, they, like all human beings, marvel at the brilliant color of the leaves, both on the trees and on the ground. This little three-line verse is a fine one for introduction of the study:

Down! Down!*

Down, down
Yellow and brown
The leaves are falling
Over the town.

Eleanor Farjeon

With a minimum of encouragement, children can add a line or two to this poem, making their own, such as:

On the ground,
And blowing all around.

The following is a good outline to use for a discussion with all of the children. More advanced children can be encouraged to use it for developing reports from research reading.

I. Trees get ready for winter.
   A. Leaves change color.
   B. Trees drop their fruit.
      1. Fruit
      2. Nuts
      3. Cones

II. Trees live all year.
   A. Next year's bud is just above the old leaf.
   B. Feeding is necessary to help trees grow.
   C. The tree's growth can be seen in a cross-section.

III. Trees are cut down.
   A. This can bring damage to community.
   B. Planting trees and restoring forests are important.

Unlimited classroom activities can take place from studying trees. *Again,* the informal, short field trip to the nearest trees provides the original stimulation. The following are a few suggested activities:

1. Carefully cut a twig from a tree where the leaf has just dropped off leaving the leaf bud just above it. Take the twig into the classroom and put it in water, thus forcing it to grow. This will show the children that the tree is not dead just because its leaves have dropped off.

2. Take the class to a tree that is losing its leaves. On a branch, put a piece of black friction tape fastening it securely. In the spring take the class back to see what is happening to the branch.

3. Have the children make a collection of nuts. This ties in closely with the activities on the seed unit. Furthermore, it can lead to discussions and research on how people, as well as animals, use nuts for food.

The following is a delightful play that fits into the nature theme and that children enjoy acting out.

Johnny and Mary Maple

Cast:	Narrator
	Other leaves (three boys reading chorally)
	Betty Birch
	Dinah Elm
	Johnny Maple (rest of the boys reading chorally)
	Mary Maple (rest of the girls reading chorally)
Narrator:	Johnny Maple and Mary Maple were two leaves that lived at the top of a tall maple tree. They could look down and see everything that was happening.
	When the firebell rang, Johnny and Mary watched the engine pull out of the firehouse. They would shout to the other leaves just where the fire was.
	When Mr. Pickard, the policeman, blew his whistle at the corner of Main and High Streets, they could see the cars stopping.
	One morning Mary called to Johnny:
Mary:	"Your shirt is turning yellow."
Johnny (laughing):	"Your blouse is turning red."
Mary:	"Mother Tree said this would happen, wonder why?"
Johnny:	"She told me it's because it is autumn. Soon we will go on a trip, too."
Mary:	"A trip?" (in surprise)
Johnny:	"Yes, look down on the ground. Already some leaves have left us."
Narrator:	The next morning when Mary woke up Johnny had gone.
Mary:	"Where are you, Johnny?"
Narrator:	But Johnny didn't answer.
Mary:	"Oh, well, soon it will be my turn to leave Mother Tree. Then I will hunt for Johnny."
Narrator:	Sure enough! That's just what happened. Along came a big gust of wind. Mary Maple waved

good-by to Mother Tree and went sailing through the air. Down, down, down, she went, till she reached the ground.

Mary (shouting):
"Hi boys! Where's Johnny Maple?"

Other Leaves:
"You'll have to hunt for him. Every time Mr. Wind blows we travel round and round trying to find our old friends."

Mary:
"What's it like down here?"

Other Leaves:
"Oh, it's fun."

Mary:
(In a hurry to find Johnny) "Hello! Hello! Have you seen Johnny?"

Betty Birch:
"I saw him yesterday."

Dinah Elm:
"I think he is on the other side of the park."

Mary:
"Come, Mr. Wind, please blow me to the other side of the park."

Narrator:
"All right," said Mr. Wind, and he blew so hard that three people lost their hats and the water in the pond splashed up on the lily leaves.

Mary:
"Johnny! Johnny!"

Johnny:
"Mary Maple! Here I am."

Mary:
"Where?" rubbing her eyes.

Johnny:
"Here."

Mary:
"But, but, but—you've lost your yellow shirt. You have a brown shirt now. And it is all stiff and starched."

Johnny:
"Look at yourself. You have a brown shirt. And it is stiff and starched, too. If it weren't, Mr. Wind couldn't blow you across the park."

Mary jumped up:
"This is fun, I like to feel the wind against my blouse. Can we play like this all winter?"

Johnny:
"Oh no, you get tired of playing all the time. Billy Poplar says the gardener will gather us up. He has an important job for us to do."

Narrator:
Mary Maple puffed out her new stiff brown blouse.

Mary:
"I like that. Is it *very* important?"

Johnny:
"Yes, indeed!" "The gardener needs us to keep the roots of the plants warm during the winter."

Mary: "I'll do my part proudly."

Johnny: "When the frost comes and the snow comes we will snuggle closer and closer to the roots."

Narrator: And that's what Mary and Johnny did.

The skillful teacher makes the most of each unit experience, stimulating children to want to relate it to other meaningful activities. Both of these units on seeds and trees can arouse interest in animals' preparation for living in winter, as well as man's harvesting and preservation of crops. The wonders of nature are forever new to boys and girls. A flexible curriculum deftly uses the children's interests to teach the secrets of natural science and what man must do to protect his environment.

And how does this teach reading? Children will learn to read from relevant experiences in which they have been personally involved: reading chorally, becoming authors by making books, writing on their own or dictating, finding answers by reading interesting books on the subject being studied,* learning the Dolch basic sight words from repetition of them in choral reading, *supplemented* by a diagnostic word study program. For example, in the one poem "Seeds" there are seventy-three words of which sixty-four are basic words that children must know instantly to be good readers. Could you make a picture for such words as "some," "are," "never," "kind"? These words are repeated in a meaningful way many times in this one poem. Repetition of these words in the poem, *with consonants underlined,* can help children recognize them in any reading material. All of these activities give purpose and enjoyment to learning the skills of reading.

---

* Excellent examples of simple, scientifically based books that are a must in the room collection of books for this unit are the *Let's Read-And-Find-Out Books,* New York: Thomas Y. Crowell Co., 1961. Some of the titles in the series are *A Tree is a Plant, How a Seed Grows,* and *Down Come the Leaves.*

CHAPTER FIVE

Unstructuring a First-Grade Teacher

Miss Mary Ellen Wollenberg's (previously mentioned in Chapter One) first-grade room was used frequently by the writer for preservice training of teachers in phonics. Later her room became a laboratory where many ideas put forth in this book were demonstrated and shown to be practical. In March 1969, discussions started between her and the writer which led to the reorganization of her teaching. The following is her story of her room before and after.

DESCRIPTION OF A PRESCRIBED BASAL
READING PROGRAM—FIRST GRADE

Our school uses a basal series which has the usual prereading readiness activities, such as learning the alphabet, sequence, picture interpretation, left to right progression—all of the general readiness activities for reading.

To help the teacher group the children for instruction, readiness tests were used to check their competency in:

1. Discrimination between likenesses and differences
2. Coordination through copy work
3. Vocabulary by marking pictures

The results give a general picture of the maturity of a child and his ability to look at the world around him. In the four years that I have taught, I have been able to make the correct predictions before the test, through observation starting the first day of school, as to which children would fall in the average, slow, or fast groups. Only a few have surprised me.

After grouping the children, they are tested at the completion of each level of skill development. For example, a test checks the child's discrimination of the letters of the alphabet, when he has completed the *readiness workbook*. Upon successfully passing the readiness achievement tests, the child uses the first *preprimer*, which introduces reading with emphasis placed on the beginning, middle, and final sounds of a word.

In all of the readers everything is centered around one family. I think that's one of the drawbacks of the program, as children don't always want to read about a family, *particularly if their own family experience is different*. In the first preprimer, as in all of the readers, there is a simplified sentence structure. Sentences convey very short thoughts. I found that the children could express themselves better orally before, than after, they had worked in the preprimers. This was true of their writing also.

A short story from one of the preprimers shows the contrived sentence structure:

> See it. See it go in. See it go up. It can come down. Oh, see it come down, down, down. Oh, Oh, I can see pretty Pete. Pretty Pete can ride it. See pretty Pete ride. Ride pretty Pete, ride, ride up, up, up, ride down, down, down.

This story is two pages long, and it is one of the last stories in the first preprimer. These short sentences are interspersed with pictures of an airplane flying and the children watching.

One of the stories from the second preprimer is about a little boy playing happily with all of his toys. Then he goes to a toy store with his mother, brother, and sister, where they see toy animals that are colorful and very nice. This is the story:

> Look Mother, I see something funny. It is a funny toy. Do you see it, Mother? See, here it is. (It's a little yellow lion that has quite a personality, but the story doesn't talk about it.) Oh, I see a funny little toy. It is brown and red. Look, see here it is. Here is the toy. Here is a big toy. See this big toy. It can play. Look, it can go. Oh, this is a funny toy. Look, see it go. Look, Mother. See me ride. I can ride the toy. I can make it go up and down. This is fun! Oh, this is fun!

Now all of the toys are exceptional toys for children. One is a little bear playing a xylophone—a pull toy; one, a rocking horse; one, a Mighty Mouse; another looks like a rubber doll that flies. No mention of them is made in the story; they're presented through pictures.

Ending sounds are further developed at the preprimer level through the use of rhyming words. After completing the preprimers the children are tested for:

1. Consonant mastery—consonants are matched with pictures.

2. Literal comprehension—stories of ten short sentences are used. Questions about each story are asked and the children circle what they think is the correct answer. An example from "Building a Dog House":

   a) Who spoke last in the story?
   b) What color was the dog house?
   c) What did the dog mean when he said "bow-wow"?
   (One of the choices is "thank-you.")

The children are permitted to go back to the story to find the answer. The child's growth in understanding and word attack is judged by these test results.

The primer and the first reader level stories continue with the same family group, sharing and living together in a happy home, where they all do things together.

The phonics program on the *primer* level begins development of understanding of all the short vowels. The teacher's manual is set up so that there is a variety of games, exercises, charts, and cards that reinforce the short vowel sound. When the children complete the primer level, they know one-syllable words that have a short vowel sound. First, the stories feature short "*a*," words, e.g., dad, can, and bag, then continue with words using the other short vowels. The *first reader* phonics program emphasizes long vowel sounds and the consonant digraphs.

Evaluation of a Traditional Reading Program

Up until this year I have always had three reading groups made up of the ones that I felt were above average, the average, and the slower ones. But this year, in order to meet the needs of the class, I have grouped as follows:

a) Lowest–two boys and one girl
b) Next to lowest—five boys

c) Next to highest—five girls and three boys
d) Highest—four girls

We really have had a hard time this year. I have realized more than ever that placing the children in ability groups makes them all unhappy. Even the faster children want to do something different and want to be in a different group. This certainly is true for the middle- and slow-group children. On the playground, I have found that children don't want to associate with those in the slow group. This feeling has carried over into everything all day. When we have mathematics, the ones that are slower in reading are afraid to raise their hands. They don't want to participate; they feel that the other children will laugh. The faster children haven't meant to brag or hurt other children's feelings, but they're always saying, "I got this," or "I got that," and "You don't have this on your paper" or "Why didn't Miss Wollenberg put an excellent on your paper?" It really becomes hard to work with children when they start discriminating against each other.

In the mornings, during group reading, the children who are not reading do seatwork at their desks, mostly from workbooks. There is a separate phonics section in the different workbooks where drill is given on consonant and vowel sounds, that is, a page of words with pictures to illustrate particular sounds which the child must find.

I used to correct the workbooks—I never let the children correct their own. The only children that I would have trusted to grade their own work were those in the highest group, but I didn't want to make this discrimination. I realize now that I should have let all of them check their seatwork, making the answer sheet available to them.

The children had been told that after finishing their workbooks, they could get a book from the bookshelf or the library to read. But did this happen? No! The "round-robin" decoding experience had not produced a desire for independent reading. The second-grade teacher told me that most of her children *still would not read the library books. They were not "readers," regardless of the fact that they could read in their circle.* That's one of the reasons I was willing to look for a new way to use our reading time.

Moreover, I didn't feel that the children were learning to read fluently. Their oral expression in reading was choppy, and, even though the words and sentences were easy, they didn't read with the spark of enjoyment. They were really beginning to dread getting out their readers, even though they liked the new stories. They never wanted to reread or go back. Their attitude showed that they were completely finished with the story once they had read it. Now that I've seen them read library and trade books, I can see why they were quite bored with the former reading program. In addition, I think they needed new ideas which the prescribed reading program was not giving them. Their background experiences weren't broad enough, and nothing in the classroom was happening to develop ideas.

Involving the Children in Choice of Time and Grouping for Reading and Other Activities

I decided to ungroup and involve the children in planning their time for reading, phonics, art, and writing.

It was really a surprise to the children when I told them they could sign up for reading at one of three specified times, choose the group they would be in, and select their book to bring to the reading circle. As well as choosing a reading group, they also were told to sign up for phonics, art, etc., as seatwork while the other children were reading.

I realize now I threw too much at them at one time. What happened was that each child signed each paper three times, as they didn't understand the idea of making choices. It took almost half an hour each day to do this. *The orderly plan that finally evolved was this:* I put up one list, they signed up once for reading at 9:00, 9:30, or 10:00. It took three weeks to get them used to this plan. Then, one Friday, I told them we would sign up to do three things in the morning. Since they had become accustomed to signing up for reading, they understood better how to sign one paper once and go to another place to sign for the other two activities, for a different time. The three activities they signed up for were reading, the "make-it" table and story writing.

Reading under the New Plan

The children were encouraged to prepare for their reading groups by having a book of their choice at their desks. Then I would call respectively for the 9:00, 9:30, or 10:00 group. At first, they would come up to the circle and sit and wait for me. I don't feel it was their fault, I feel it was my fault and really the fault of the reading program that we had been using which *made everything center on the teacher.* I had to say, "Let's look at the book. Let's look at the title. Who wrote the book? What do you think it's about?" All of these things they should have done out of desire, eagerness, and curiosity. They finally would open the book and wait—each one would wait—for his turn to sit next to me and read to me quietly. They wanted me to hear them read. At first their only thought was *for me to hear them read orally.* I told them they didn't need me—that they had to do this on their own, but if they really needed me to help, I would. Finally, some of the children who had a stronger desire to read than others started on their own and finished a book. Gradually their example was followed by others. After they became familiar with the plan and involved with self-selection of books, each group read about half an hour to forty minutes daily. For the first ten or fifteen minutes they hardly even talked to me. They didn't even look up. They kept their noses in their books. They would go over what they had read the day before, or they'd look at the ending and try to figure out what was going to happen in between, and they began to read! *You could tell when they really settled down to work at it.* Keeping individual records of each child's reading progress on index cards is important. As a child talked or read to me or as I watched him read or observed what he chose, I made note of it on his card so I could later evaluate his progress. These observations helped me to plan meaningful word study programs for another time in the day.

Resolving Problems with the New Reading Plan

In my inexperience with the new type of reading organization, at first I chose books for the children from the library that were too hard for many of them. As I recognized this, I gradually withdrew the more difficult ones and put easier ones in their place. I interspersed the library books with simple trade books and supplementary basals that had not been used in our previous basal reading program.

Under the new plan of reading, I discovered how badly some children's self-concepts had been damaged by having been placed in a low reading group in our former reading program. At first they chose books that were far too difficult. To deal with this problem, I learned that I must search for books written at the preprimer and primer level which had colorful pictures and short interesting stories. It must be remembered that no child can make progress in reading when he is allowed to choose books too difficult for him. To make these easier books acceptable to the slower-reading child, I would take them to the reading circle and introduce them to the whole group, after which I would suggest that Bruce, Ann, or whoever else in the group needed a book at that level, read the book. By being enthusiastic about certain pictures, I was able to create interest among all in the simpler book. It was suggested that the child reading the book tell the others about the story later.

Of course, there were times when some children chose simple books out of laziness; then again, they'd pick a book with big words in it. However, in general, I would say they began to choose books that they could read or that were just a little bit hard for them—so they could feel they had accomplished something.

I had one little boy who poked around and poked around, but he finally read two or three very good books. His nature was to get out of everything the easy way; so he had to pick all the easy books first. He got to the point where he was tired of them. Maybe he had to go through that to discover how to find a story that he'd enjoy.

Soon all of the children began to select books that were more appropriate for their reading level. It's amazing how the new plan worked itself out with very little guidance from me.

The Children Found Favorite Books

One book in the room that everyone was crazy about was *Old Rosey, The Horse That Nobody Understood.** It was a long book and every page had almost solid print with a picture on the other side. It was a conversational book; the horse and the farmer always talked. This is the first page:

> What a day it was going to be. Farmer Dilly did not know it, his old horse Rosey did not know it and it was a good thing, too. "Now you see here, Rosey," said Farmer Dilly, "we must get to the milk train on time today. Do you understand?" Rosey's head went up and down. "Nothing silly like yesterday," said the farmer. Rosey shook her head. "And nothing like the day before that." Rosey's big brown eyes seemed to say, "Who me?"

Every time the children read that book there was joy in their faces; the love of the book, the accomplishment of what they had done reading these ideas made them happy all day long.

Another book that was a favorite of the children was about colors: the colors of the world, the colors in things. This book was called *Red is Never a Mouse.*** It was about all the things we know that have a certain color, but it was a humorous book; it had readers imagine qualities that would not be true of familiar things, such as an orange whale or a purple goat. It rhymed and the words and the structure were unique:

> Do you know what blue is? Blue is a jay or a bottle of ink. Blue is a berry you eat in a wink. Blue is the river or winning first prize. Blue is a bluebell or clear summer skies. Blue is the water for sailing a boat. But blue is never, no never, a goat!

---

* Moore, Lilian and Leone Adelson, *Old Rosey, The Horse That Nobody Understood,* Eau Claire, Wisconsin: E. M. Hale and Company, 1952.

** Clifford, Eth, *Red Is Never a Mouse,* Indianapolis: Bobbs-Merrill Company, Inc., 1960.

Writing Develops from Wide Reading

Their reading affected their writing and the way they began to think. They didn't think in short sentences all the time. They thought in connected ideas and were able to say more than "It is red." They'd say "It's red and it's coming fast!" The children began writing about things that we had fun discussing. This started by *expanding sentences*. For example, I would put on the board: "Poodle ran." After getting the children involved, it became, "The curly little poodle ran into the golden cage." Then they thought of other words for curly: fuzzy, stringy, etc. Cage became "the black trap" or some other descriptive term. Last, they each wrote their version of the final sentence. This way the children developed use of vocabulary that helped their sentences express color and feeling. They no longer wrote about just a "butterfly," but about a "yellow buterfly" or a "lady butterfly" or a "happy butterfly." They used words to give the butterfly a little life and personality. Wide reading in a variety of books gave them ideas for their own story writing. Finally, the "make-it" table became the place to finish their books by designing an appropriate book cover.

Informal Phonics Study

After sign-up in the morning, we would talk about a problem relating to phonics, for example, words with double o—pool, hook. The two sounds of oo would be discussed. The children would then be encouraged to pronounce words containing these sounds, using initial and terminal consonants as aids to saying a word that made sense. I would put ten or fifteen words on the board for them to pronounce. With this practice they were not afraid to attack words containing a double o in their independent reading.

Another approach I used with the children helped them with new words in their reading. I wrote sentences to them on the board every day leaving out the vowel letters. One day I wrote "G––d m–rn–ng, b––s –nd g–rls, I h–p– y–u h–v– a h–pp– d––." At least ten could read it immediately. The other children didn't know exactly what they were supposed to do, but the next day, more of them understood. Every day I had similar "coded" messages on the board for them to read, using consonant-context. Eventually most of the children could figure them out. They began enjoying this game, and it carried over to their independent reading. Words that would have stopped them, because of their complex vowel sounds, became less of a problem as they learned to read for meaning depending upon the consonants.

Happy Results

As the new plan became thoroughly understood, the children grew happier! They knew what to do; they knew where to sign up; they knew what book they wanted to read. They felt the adventure of finding another book. Every week I'd put in ten new books so that there finally were sixty interesting books in the library corner. The children sought out the ones they knew came from the library because there was a prestige symbol attached to them.

Parents began questioning "What is this that the children are always talking about? Why do they always want to read at home?" One mother asked why were we not having regular reading groups? Her little boy had told her that we didn't need groups any more because, "That was for first graders—now we're getting ready for second grade."

One time at lunch, when all the little children eat together, some of the first graders asked the second graders if they had ever read *The Story About Ping.** One of the second graders said, "No, I never heard of it." The little first grader was very surprised that he had never taken it out of the library, since it had been there "the whole time." The second graders began to wonder what was up. The first graders knew about the library books, and they didn't. It helped all to see that to read is really quite an important thing in life.

I can't say that there's one thing in this reading program that wasn't excellent for the children. As for me, I felt that I was so much freer. Now I could really work with the children. I wasn't telling them what to look for, telling this and telling that. They were learning on their own. I became a director, not the one doing all of the work and handing it out to them. I think that if children can learn to take responsibility early in their lives, they really will have the key to successful education.

SKILLS CHECKLISTS FOR TEACHER'S SELF-ANALYSIS

The checklists which appear on the following pages summarize the techniques put forth in this book for development of language, reading, and perceptual motor skills. These checklists were circulated among former students of the writer. The comments which appear herein are those of two students, one who is now a first-grade teacher and the other a kindergarten teacher.

---

* Flack, Marjorie and Kurt Wiese, *The Story about Ping* New York: Viking Press, 1933.

Language and Reading Skills Development, Checklist for the Teacher

	First-grade teacher*		Kindergarten teacher	
	Regularly	Comments	Regularly	Comments
I. Making children authors by:				
A. Providing relevant experience daily to motivate children to want to communicate about them in writing.	X			
B. Taking dictation from individual children.	X	"This is possible in any classroom."	X	"Using fifth- and sixth-grade pupils once a week to help take dictation is an ideal way to carry out this activity, which benefits all. I also use parent aides."
C. Providing an atmosphere in which children who are ready to do so are supported in their own efforts to write independently.	X			
D. Making books from children's stories.	X	"We have more of our 'own' books than those from the library!"	X	
1. Allowing children to illustrate them.	X		X	

* Charlene Ewald, Northern Michigan University Graduate 1969.
** Barbara Gratsch, Northern Michigan University Graduate 1969.

	Kindergarten teacher		First-grade teacher	
	Regularly	Comments	Regularly	Comments
II. Helping children grow into reading by:				
A. Using choral reading on a daily basis with all children having a copy of the poem or story so that they are able to correlate phonemes and graphemes.	—		X	
B. Using expansion of kernel sentences with participation of the entire class to help all children develop syntax and vocabulary from their own language.	—		X	"We develop class books from these, also."
C. Interpreting to children the idea that reading can be "talk written down," discussion of pictures, as well as reading stories in books.	X	"I find that the set of *Kinder/Owl Books* by Holt, Rinehart and Winston can be easily adapted to this use."	X	
D. Developing critical thinking by asking open-ended questions when using choral reading, sentence expansion, unit study reading, and the weekly classroom newspaper.	X		X	

	First-grade teacher		Kindergarten teacher	
	Regularly	Comments	Regularly	Comments
III. Reading groups arranged by:				
A. Allowing children to select the time of day and group of their choice.	X			
B. Rotating their sitting next to you in the group of their choice, so each may read individually to you for diagnostic purposes.	X	"Even conferences (individual) for 4 minutes are very helpful."		
IV. Word study program developed by:				
A. Having a *separate time from reading* each day in which you group children with similar problems to study phoneme-grapheme relationships and word structure.	X			
1. Making provision, via a tape recorder, for developing auditory discrimination of sounds, particularly the short vowels.	X	"The children also can use sign-up for this—once a particular time is set for it."	X	"Occasionally"
2. Reinforcing the word study time *with writing, remembering* that there is a closer relationship between phonics and writing than phonics and reading.	X			

	First-grade teacher		Kindergarten teacher	
	Regularly	Comments	Regularly	Comments
B. Using consonant-context (placing dashes for vowels in words) to reinforce consonant sounds in initial, terminal, and medial position, as well as a method to increase reading for meaning.	X	"The children love the challenge, also!"	—	
V. Relevant curriculum via unit teaching provided by:				
A. Giving your children wide experiences which will lead to self-initiated learning (within the framework of the social study and science curriculum).	X	"Makes it more interesting for everyone to study units."	X	"Personal involvement in learning processes produces happy children. Self-selection and pacing require more work on the teacher's part but result in rewarding outcomes. Over half of the children in my room, who have experienced freedom of choice, are actually reading and writing their own stories. Those who cannot read still feel
B. Allowing children to become personally involved in the learning process, making individual and group plans for carrying through on projects—within the framework of the school curriculum, giving them "freedom to learn" as contrasted with teacher-prescribed activities.	X		X	

	First-grade teacher		Kindergarten teacher	
	Regularly	Comments	Regularly	Comments
C. Providing books at varying reading levels on the chosen unit of study so that all children can participate in reading and gathering information. (To accomplish this the assistance of the librarian within the school, city, or state must be obtained.)		"Yes, first graders *can* use a library."	—	good about their achievements, since they select their own projects, contribute to group activities according to their levels of capacity, and feel a part of the class."
D. Helping children develop skills in outlining and note taking so that they will be able to organize facts to use in meaningful oral and written reports.	X	"Occasionally"	—	

Physical Activities for Perceptual-Motor Skills Development, Checklist for the Teacher

	First-grade teacher		Kindergarten teacher	
	Regularly	Comments	Regularly	Comments
VI. Interspersing the day's activities with meaningful physical exercise by:*				"*Success Through Play*** helps me plan the physical activities I use."

	First-grade teacher		Kindergarten teacher	
	Regularly	Comments	Regularly	Comments
A. Developing balance and posture by using a walking board, balance beam, and jumping exercises.	X		X	
B. Locomotion (movement of body through space without thinking of manipulative skills involved.	X			
1. Laterality—using games to develop each child's ability to identify body parts: awareness of left, right, front, back, up, down, within the child's body; differentiating between left and right side.	X	"Pasting or taping outlines of both right and left hands on desk top, with words 'right' and 'left' written on them were helpful with my classes."	X	
Examples a) Angels-in-the-snow b) Games using left and right hands or feet				
2. Directionality—using games to develop each child's awareness	X	"Especially at the beginning of the year."		

* Ideas for chart based primarily upon techniques described in *The Slow Learner in the Classroom* by Newell C. Kephart, Columbus, Ohio: Charles E. Merrill Publishing Co., 1971. Used by permission.
** Radler, D. H. and N. C. Kephart, *Success Through Play*, New York: Harper and Row, 1960.

| | Kindergarten teacher | | First-grade teacher | |
	Regularly	Comments	Regularly	Comments
of left, right, front, back, etc., in the world around him.	X		X	
Examples				
a) Obstacle race				
b) Crab walk—children move in any direction upon command				
c) Hopscotch				
d) Skip				
e) Interpreting rhythm to music, holding position upon command				
C. Contact (involves reach, grasp, release).	X		—	"Occasionally. Would have been better if we had the use of a gymnasium."
1. Ball-handling.				
Examples				
a) Bounce, kick, throw—beanbags are good in-door ball substitutes for kicking and throwing.				
2. Rhythms and dances requiring:				"Clapping out rhythms is great."
a. Clapping hands				

	First-grade teacher		Kindergarten teacher	
	Regularly	Comments	Regularly	Comments
b. Movement with scarves or fans, etc.	X		X	
D. Receipt and propulsion—ability to control moving objects toward and away from self:				
1. Hit, bounce, and catch.	X		X	
Example				
a) Measure off five feet from wall and draw a line on the floor. Draw a line on the wall with chalk as high as children's knees. The child must hit the wall above the line with the ball, let it bounce once and catch it. Let each do it as fast as possible for a limited time.				
VII. Incorporating activities to develop children's perceptual-motor match through:				
A. Chalkboard activities:				
1. Making circles, using preferred hand.	X	"This has helped some children very much."	X	

	First-grade teacher		Kindergarten teacher	
	Regularly	Comments	Regularly	Comments
2. Making double circles using both hands simultaneously.	X		X	
3. Practicing manuscript writing.	X		X	
B. Form perception activities—development of visual constancy of size and shape:				
1. Sorting according to shape, using the circle, square and triangle.	X		X	
Example				
a) Reproducing shapes on paper.	X		X	
2. Sorting objects according to their differences and similarities in size and shape.	X		X	
Examples				
a) Sorting buttons, rocks, seeds, dried peas and beans				
b) Assembling puzzles, etc.				
c) Stringing wooden beads in accordance to a pattern				

	First-grade teacher		Kindergarten teacher	
	Regularly	Comments	Regularly	Comments
3. Cutting, placing, sewing, and pasting.	X	"Very good!"	X	
C. Ocular control. *Examples*				
1. Having children hold their heads straight and still, while moving from left to right a large bead along a wire or string which is about five feet in front of them.		"Occasionally"		
2. Using a suspended ball (or other object) for a child's practice in focusing and following the object with both eyes at once while holding his head still.	X		X	

93

CHAPTER SIX

One Answer
Versus Thinking

Little Boxes*

Little boxes on the hillside, little boxes made of ticky tacky,
Little boxes, little boxes, little boxes all the same
There's a green one and a pink one and a blue one
  and a yellow one,
And they're all made out of ticky tacky,
  and they all look just the same.

Keep the bell of freedom ringing!

Do we do it with workbooks where one answer is correct or by setting up situations where children can think and develop independent thought?

Reading is a process; there is no content in mere sounds and symbols. Content develops when sounds and symbols are used to convey meaning through such contexts as social studies, science, literature, mathematics, and poetry. Children must be helped to get *beyond* the mere decoding process. They must be led to understand that written words are important only as they are used to convey thoughts, develop aesthetics, and solve problems. Without this kind of "open" learning atmosphere in the classroom, children are deprived of freedom to think. Workbooks and oral questions that demand *one correct answer* soon condition them to think alike, and they become confined to "little boxes."

Teachers should grasp every opportunity to develop classroom respect for independent thinking. Children should be allowed to get together, compare and argue over their answers, and disagree if they can produce logical answers. This idea contrasts sharply with the usual procedure of children doing workbook exercises where *one answer only* is correct. A confining procedure such as the latter causes conscientious teachers to spend hours checking workbooks with red pencils, looking for *the one answer* supplied by the teacher's edition.

---

* Words and music Malvina Reynolds, Copyright © 1962 by Schroder Music Co. (ASCAP) Used by permission.

DEVELOPMENT OF LOGICAL SEQUENCE

One of the first steps toward the goal of independent thought in the classroom is developing the basic skill of sequential thinking. Does a workbook exercise on sequence, done quietly by the child at his seat, develop critical thinking? The position being put forth here is that development of critical thinking requires discussion with others—interchange of ideas—and finally independent thought. In such an atmosphere children will see that there are many different logical ways to arrive at a decision.

Sets of Related Pictures Stimulate Discussion

The use of different sets of related pictures has proven to be an effective way to develop readiness for sequential thinking. Six is a manageable number to use. However, before the pictures are presented, the idea of numbering items from one to six has to be developed with kindergarteners and first graders. The child has to understand the numerical order of 1, 2, 3, 4, 5, and 6 in order to be able to number his pictures after deciding the order to use in telling a story about them. *Having made his own decision* regarding the pictures, he must then place a numeral on each picture starting with one and going to six to show the order of the story he will tell or write.

After this numerical concept has been established, the teacher is ready to use imagination in presenting, for the children to manipulate, sets of pictures portraying different cycles of life or events. Lively discussions in which children give different reasons for varying order should be encouraged.

Examples of Pictures for this Activity

1. A boy fishing, water, a boat, fishing equipment, pail, worms
2. A young boy sleeping, stretching, washing, eating, brushing his teeth, and going to school
3. Variations of a "seed" motif sequence can be utilized:
   a. Fertilizer, grass, seed, long grass, lawnmower, and man
   b. Seeds, watering can, apple tree, apple, apple pie, and little girl
   c. Seed, earth, sun, rain, little tree, and big tree
   d. Seed, small plant, vase, large plant, plant with buds, and plant with flowers
   e. Seed, small tree, large tree, apple blossoms, tree with many apples, and basket full of apples
   f. Seed, sun, rain, sprout, plant with flowers, and vase of flowers
   g. Boy eating apple, core on ground, seed from core on ground, tree blossoms, tree with apples, boy picking apple

h. Acorn, acorn buried by squirrel, rain, roots and sprouts on acorn, small oak tree, and large oak tree

4. A bare tree branch, branch with leaves, a branch with leaves and apples, a branch with colored leaves, leaves on the ground, basket

5. Family eating breakfast, children playing outside, eating lunch, eating snacks, children at school, and children ready for bed

6. Colored leaves on trees, a hunter, a dog, three puppies, a rabbit, a gun

If children are told that many different stories can be made from any set of pictures, they can be inspired to become "authors" writing (dictating) their own stories. However, some children need a great deal of experience in arranging and rearranging pictures before they can arrive at the desired goal of logical independent thinking.

As stated so well in *Language Experiences in Reading, Teacher's Resource Book, Level I,* p. 208:*

1. A sequence of events or ideas can be identified in good stories.

2. The same pictures suggest different ideas to different people.

The book suggests giving children six pictures—relating to a mother bird—for manipulation and discussion.

Sequence Book Project Developed from Bird Pictures

An interesting project can be developed when children use these pictures in a six-page booklet, cutting and pasting one picture on each page in the order that seems logical to the child, and then writing about it.**

An experience with 112 first- and second-grade children doing the project revealed the following statistics: eleven used traditional*** sequential thinking, seventy-one developed a logical creative sequence, and

---

* Allen, Roach Van and Claryce Allen, Chicago, Ill.: Encyclopedia Britannica Press, 1966. Used by permission.

** If each child's respect for *his own ability to think* and *act independently* has *not been established* sufficiently in the classroom, it is advisable to separate children as they work on the sequence booklet project to encourage individuality. All should be reassured that there is *no one way* to develop the booklet; that it will be fun to surprise each other at the completion of the project by reading the books aloud to show the different ways each one figures out his story.

*** Traditional sequence of the six bird pictures as defined here is 1) the mother bird, 2) the nest is built, 3) the eggs are laid, 4) the eggs crack open as they are hatched, 5) hungry babies are in the nest, 6) the mother bird gets worms to feed them.

Donald writes his story about the birds

thirty showed that they did not have an adequate understanding of sequence.

Can you imagine a workbook allowing *different correct answers?*

The following pages show examples of first-grade stories. Before reading the children's stories—study the pictures yourself and see what your answer would be!

The bird is a big mother. The mother bird has hair.

The mother bird made the nest of hair.

The mother bird flew up in the tree.

The mother bird put the eggs in the nest.

The baby birds hatched in the morning out of the eggs.

They flew down to their mother in the path.

The eggs are hatching

The birds are trying to fly

The mama bird is gettnig some worms

now they are
eating The
worms.

now they
are gone
flying

now they
live HaPPY
ever after.

Scott

ABOUT BIRDS

One day There was a Robin he was beautiful and nice one day he was flying when he   saw a nest, there was   nothing in it so he Usde   it.   It was very comfortable so he picked it To hatch Some eggs. Then she   snuggled down and stayd   there.

for   a long, longtime it was very, very cold at night he ~~we~~ w

2

Scott's unfinished story was found in the wastebasket at the end of a writing period. It is included here as an illustration of the frustration that a sensitive and capable first-grade child can feel when he is rushed to finish a project. He had a great deal to say and was able to write it independently of the teacher. As pointed out in Chapter Three, a child needs to feel that time is unlimited as he pursues a project. Rigid time schedules interfere with creativity.

Scott was not only unable to finish his story in the allotted time, but he was not called upon afterwards to read his story. Several other children were. This may have been an additional factor in his throwing the story into the wastebasket—a feeling that his efforts were useless.

It is very important that each child get to read his story. The children can be told to bring them to the reading circle to share with teammates. However, group reading of the stories should be delayed until the next day to allow the slower writers time to finish their stories. The plan of reading in small groups is preferable to having stories read before the entire class. Restlessness is likely to result in listening to thirty versions of the same theme!

Sequence Book Project Developed from Pictures Relating to Squirrels

On page 108 is another set of six pictures. What kind of a story would you tell from them?

The stories that follow show that first-grade children had no trouble in developing many stories from these pictures in good sequential order.*

Making good use of opportunities similar to this in teaching sequence will contribute to independent solving of other problems.

---

* These stories are written in i.t.a.

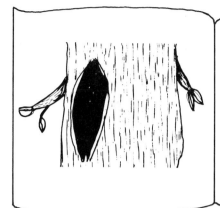

the skwirrel
hoel.

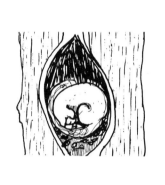

the skwirrel
is sleeping.

the skwirrel
is on the
tree.

hee is
eetirg
    nuts.

the skwirrel
found nuts.

Shee feeds
her baebys.

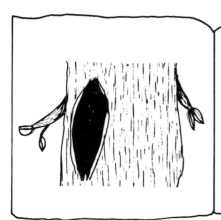

this is a tree.

the skwirrel eets nuts.

the skwirrel is jumping for sum nuts.

the skwirrel
is on the
branch.

the skwirrel
is feedirg
her baebys.

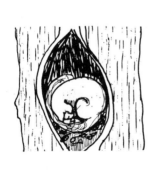

the skwirrel
is hiebernæting.

CHAPTER SEVEN

Using the Laboratory Experience Method with the Disadvantaged Child

What is a disadvantaged child? Many different answers can be given. It *cannot* truthfully be said, however, that disadvantaged children live in any particular location. There may be a higher concentration of them in certain areas, namely the ghettoes, but they are in some number in *every* classroom in the United States. In this chapter, the disadvantaged child is defined as one who has the capacity to learn but is faced with any number of the following problems in his home:

1. Home life is unstable, usually with only one parent. If both parents live together, there is much tension because of their incompatability. He feels that he is an unwanted child.

2. There is usually no one at home when the child returns from school. Often no one helps the child get ready for school.

3. Meals are irregular without the family gathering together as a group. Frequently the child goes to school with little or no breakfast. This is not necessarily related to economics!

4. Malnutrition causes frequent illnesses and absences from school.

5. Language differs from standard usage. (School language)

6. There is very little communication among members of the family.

7. Television is the center of the home. Children are allowed to watch any program of their choice and stay up late at night for viewing.

8. There are few books in the home, no reading is done to the children.

9. Homes often have inadequate sanitation facilities.

10. Poor economic status may cause children to be inadequately clothed.

11. Little attention is paid to children's academic progress *on a daily basis* by parents; *harsh treatment is given for failing grades.*

What a responsibility these problems place upon the school! Are these children going to be interested in books portraying happy family life? Are they going to be able to participate in usual class discussions? Are they going to know how to get along with other children, how to share, take turns—when most of what they have heard and known has been either fighting and turmoil or no family communication?

Nevertheless, basically all primary children, particularly first graders, want to learn, and their parents really want them to have an education. Since these eleven obstacles to children's success in school exist at least to some degree for so many, a tremendous responsibility is shifted to the schools. *These children are not unteachables.* The problem to be solved is many-sided:

1. A continuation of generations of untrained culturally disadvantaged people must be stopped.

2. Unstable home situations must be met with a school environment which will give children emotional security.

3. The school environment must be one that can pace children *without damaging their self-concepts,* especially those who are disadvantaged because of slow maturation, a perceptual-motor developmental lag, or other physiological problems.

4. Nutritional needs of children must be met.

5. Schools must learn how to involve parents in meaningful ways in their children's education. To succeed in the program that must be launched will require nonprofessional assistants in the classrooms. Many parents, regardless of economics or ethnic origin, would welcome being involved in school programs as helpers if properly approached.

The laboratory-unit approach to learning is the medium for giving disadvantaged children continuous learning experiences. Why? Millard H. Black* says:

> A significant body of research into the abilities of culturally disadvantaged children to communicate establishes this: these children do not listen as well as do more advantaged children; they do not speak as well; they do not read as well; nor do they write as well. . . . [In the language-experience approach] all reading instruction centers around the oral language of the pupils; these children read materials which are meaningful because they have talked about an experience and, after talking about it, have either dictated a story to the teacher—as individual or group experience stories—or have actually done the writing. . . . It is an attempt to develop a meaningful reading curriculum from the daily experiences of the pupils themselves, providing them with an opportunity to develop their listening, speaking, reading, and writing vocabularies out of things and activities with which they have immediate contact (2).

With this approach, the school embraces the children *where they are* and *goes from there* with relevant learning experiences. The "home-rooted" language (5) or "organic" language (1)—colorfully so named by Sylvia Ashton-Warner—is accepted in the classroom. With the use of choral reading of poetry, this language will gradually change as children's ears are filled with beautiful language in which they are involved personally.

Traditional graded teaching is unlikely to succeed in a classroom in which there are disadvantaged children. Teachers must be knowledgeable in designing a reading skills program related to the needs of individual students. The teachers who will succeed with these children are ones who are *not concerned with the results of standardized reading tests.* They know and understand that results will come slowly and that abundant enriching experiences must first be provided within and outside the classroom. *All learning must be relevant* and children must have been involved in its development. Procedures set forth in Chapters Two, Three, and Four provide guidelines for such teaching.

CLASSROOM CASE STUDIES

Two case studies follow which substantiate the introductory statements of this chapter. One is the experience of a student teacher working

---

* Los Angeles City Schools

with white children; the other is the experience, although brief, of the writer working with black children in a Detroit ghetto school.

STUDENT TEACHER'S REPORT*

As a student teacher, I was involved with sixty first-grade children for a period of eight weeks from April through June 1969. These children were experiencing a newly established program of team teaching, for which they were divided into four groups. Each group followed its respective schedule of classes and was involved with four teachers each day. The basis of the children's group division was focused on their reading achievement levels.

My first four weeks were spent with groups three and four, in all subject areas. The instructional reading levels were low first grade and primer.

Many of these children had serious home difficulties which influenced their self-images and personal relationships with both teachers and classmates. The economic status of the families was low. Fathers were unemployed, and in most cases the mothers were working on part-time jobs. Many families were being supported entirely through welfare aid. There were many absences and frequent colds among the children. Most of them prepared themselves for school and, therefore, were not dressed according to weather conditions. When they arrived at school, they were longing for someone to talk with—someone who listened, comforted or praised them, and accepted their small gifts with genuine appreciation.

Regardless of the problems present, it is the teacher's responsibility to improve children's self-images and desires to learn. Because of my university laboratory teaching in the language-experience approach to reading, I could think of no better program with which to help these children.

In both groups, the children were very bored in their reading periods and cared little about the stories in the basal texts. I began to involve them in acting out the stories, finding this to be successful in many ways.

First, it kept their interest in the story. Then, as each child identified with the particular character, he was able to read the lines fluently with few mistakes. Thus expressive reading began. Once the reading period

---

* Charlene Ewald, 1969 graduate, Northern Michigan University.

was more enjoyable, I began small projects. I added language-experience activities to the existing program.

To introduce the idea of authorship, and for a needed strengthening of beginning consonants, the children made alphabet books. Two pages were given for each letter of the alphabet. As the children wrote the letters on the pages, they drew an illustration of a word beginning with that letter. Because some children finished sooner than others, there was time for individual dictation of words beginning with "favorite" letters. For example, if "m" was the favorite letter, I was asked to spell "manners." Once I had written their dictated word, the child always copied it again, then thought of another word. This activity inspired them for authorship.

Each class was to make a special project which would be presented at a parent meeting. This provided an opportunity to make books of the children's stories.

Working in small groups, each child dictated a story as I wrote it on large paper. I then typed the stories on a primary typewriter and pasted the sentences on pages of cloth-covered books. Because of the expense of contact paper, I used scraps of material and Kodak dry mount paper to make hard cover books. The pages were stitched on a sewing machine. As I returned the books, each child drew his own illustration. We then used the finished books for our reading groups. On those days, the attention spans were long and the enthusiasm high. Each child felt special pride as his story was read and discussed. They could hardly wait to write more.

The class helped arrange the book display for the visiting parents. I then asked them to help me write a story which would explain how they made their books. As they sat around me dictating sentences, the children learned not to interrupt when others were speaking. They were interacting and no longer felt like the "slow groups three and four."

Then came the problem for which I was not prepared. Out of 120 first-grade parents, only sixteen came to see their children's books. I realize that there were many reasons for the parents' poor attendance. These reasons, however, are not easily understood by children. When I suggested that they take their books home, most of the children did not want to. They said no one cared if they wrote books; so they never wanted to write again. One girl, who previously had not liked school, confided to me that her father had already burned her alphabet book because there were too many school papers around their home. For fear her story would be thrown away, she wanted me to keep it.

When I realized how these children had been hurt, I suggested that we build our own room library from their books, and each week we could write different kinds of books. We cleared a book shelf and this became their library. These books were used when I read to them, for extra books in their reading groups, and for their free time reading. Once again their enthusiasm was kindled.

When I began teaching science to the entire class, I developed a unit with the children on baby animals in the spring. I decided to continue our writing experiences. After normal class discussions, filmstrips, and stories, the children drew pictures of the developmental stages of each animal under discussion. These pages were kept for the formation of a book.

At the close of each week, the children discussed what they had learned, then dictated stories about each animal. This provided me with a way of testing what they had learned and how thorough my teaching had been. I typed each of their stories as they wrote them, and kept them in folders with their illustrations.

Until this time, the science teacher was not in favor of these activities, thinking they should be saved for the language-arts-reading period. When she witnessed the entire atmosphere of the classroom and the attentiveness and eagerness these children displayed, she changed her outlook. She told me that when she previously had made different types of books with them, giving out mimeographed inserts, the children had thrown them into the wastebasket. This time they were added to our library shelf. This was because the children wrote the books themselves. Maybe the books did not look as neat and they may have taken more class time, but it was not wasted time—there was always learning going on. Most of all, these children's reading skills were improving.

The children had been exposed to much choral reading before I came to the school, and we enjoyed its use whenever possible. It was surprising how two or three poems may be enjoyed in choral speaking while preparing for recess or lunch.

When unexpected events happened—Julie brought her new kitten to class—there was no need to get upset because they were added to the children's experiences. We looked at the kitten's feet and described how they were made to help kittens walk quietly. We watched her play with string and balls, and the children touched her soft fur. I then placed the following sentence on the chalkboard:

"The kitten has fur and special feet. It likes to jump and play with us."

I showed the children how we could add new words to the sentence which might be better than those which I used. Just between the words "the" and "kitten," the children added over thirty different words to describe the kitten. Later, this developed into writing a story on the chalkboard as they dictated sentences to me. They made individual drawings of the kitten from the story we had written together. Later I mimeographed copies of the story. The children took turns reading it, and even the most immature readers read it with ease. Most of the class took the picture and story home, which pleased me very much.

Because the children had so many favorite poems for choral reading, I began making copies for them to have during the summer. We made individual poetry books, and as we added pages we read the poems and made up actions for each. Included were blank pages where the children began writing their own poems during class and, hopefully, this activity would be carried on during the summer.

As I thought back I realized I had experienced only minor discipline problems. The family problems which bothered the children only made them more responsive to the teacher's help. Some of their stories displayed startling things about their home life, but no one was made to feel ashamed. Many problems were not even known to the teacher until the children wrote about them. So often adults write letters to "get a problem off their minds," so why shouldn't children be able to do this, too?

THE WRITER'S EXPERIENCE IN TEACHING
INNER-CITY CHILDREN IN DETROIT

During the week of March 30, 1970, arrangements were made through the University of Michigan Urban Program in Education for me to introduce learning laboratory teaching to a class of Primary One children in the inner city. Time permitted me to spend only four and one-half days with the class.

The class I was given had an enrollment of twenty-seven children who had been grouped for instruction as the slowest learning children in the first grade. Despite the attempt to group these children homogeneously, their reading ability ranged from nonreaders to primer level. Thus, the traditional three reading groups were in operation in the room.

The total class consisted of twenty-six black children and one white child. Their teacher was black. The sex distribution was fifteen boys and twelve girls whose ages ranged from six to nine years. The teacher had originally been assigned thirty-five children, but as children moved from the school district no additional assignments were made to the room, mainly because these children were, on the whole, very unstable and difficult to manage. From my observation I would say that the older ones had perceptual-motor problems. None of them seemed inadequate in intelligence. Despite all of the children's problems, the teacher had developed good room control in a positive way.

Before starting to work with the children I observed their teacher's methods for one morning. She followed closely the prescribed methods of teaching reading. The main difference of the basal that she used from the other traditional basal programs was that the series had been developed with pictures showing children of different races with black children in predominance. Her three reading groups were each presented with pretaught words as prescribed by the manual. Oral reading within the group was done by the "round-robin" method with the other children required to listen as one child read orally. She did an outstanding job of getting the children to discuss the story following the silent and oral reading within each group. After their group experience, the children in the fastest group returned to their seats and obediently worked in their workbooks as directed. The other two groups were unable to keep themselves occupied and were quite restless except when reading to her in their group.

The teacher spent approximately forty-five minutes teaching word study at the beginning of the morning program. She used the Durrell-Murphy *Speech-to-Print* program as her guide for this and involved the whole class simultaneously. She showed extreme capability in keeping their interest and in making even the slow ones feel success. During the word study instruction she taught and reviewed various aspects of structural analysis: using the apostrophe both in contractions and possessives, adding the inflectional suffixes "ing" and "ed" to verbs. Her last few minutes were spent in introducing the phonograms "ear" and "all" with the use of initial consonant substitution.

The latter was to be used as part of the children's seatwork while she met with different reading groups. In addition the children were to copy sentences from the board and draw pictures to illustrate each.*

As the teacher and I worked with the children later, in writing stories, we found they were unable to apply to their writing the word study skills thus drilled and practiced.

The children were instructed to get a library book when they finished the seatwork, while waiting their turn to go to the reading circle. It was obvious that the library books had little meaning to the children

---

* It is customary for primary grade teachers to place instructions—as well as the seatwork to be done—on the chalkboard. For many children, particularly grades K-2, this practice presents grave problems. It overlooks the fact that many children's eyes have not stabilized. Inaccurate copy work will result. Each child should have a mimeographed copy of seatwork to be done, which can be placed on each desk.

except as an opportunity to get out of their seats and walk to the library shelf as often as possible. When I looked over the library books, I realized the reason for the children's lack of interest. They were far too difficult for the children to read; after quickly looking through the pictures, they were ready for another one.

TAKING OVER THE CLASS

I was most fortunate in being given an opportunity to work in J. School. The administrators wanted learning to be relevant, and the children to be personally involved in the learning process. Knowing this, I was comfortable and free to use the methods that I feel accomplish these goals.

The following describes the procedures I used to get the children personally involved.

Children Choose Their Own Groups

I explained to the children that we were going to work in teams and that each could sign up for the team of his choice: Team 1—Team 2—Team 3. I had prepared three separate sheets of chart paper with these headings and had placed numerals down the left-hand side, one to nine. These three sheets had been taped, for the children's signatures, to the chalkboard. Children who are presented with this new kind of organization need direction in its accomplishment. On the whole, however, the new groups were formed with a minimum of confusion. In later evaluating it with the room teacher, she suggested it could have been made more simple by having the children count themselves off by threes and then go to the appropriate chart to sign their names. While this suggestion would have produced more order and saved time, it would have cut down on freedom of choice for children in selecting team members.

Choral Reading

The children were called to the front of the room to be introduced to choral reading, a completely new experience for them. This activity took place twice daily thereafter. Booklets, with poetry on nine mimeographed sheets, had been prepared. The children had no idea what was meant by choral reading. When questioned as to what it was, they answered over and over "reading softly." Since children get the idea quickest by singing a song it was introduced with "Three Blind Mice." The next step was to get the children to listen to the selection that was to be read chorally, leaving out rhyming words for them to supply. Immediately, I found that these children had practically no concept of rhyming words. This is certainly understandable as their personal language (dialect) for the most part ignores ending phonemes. We worked on this all week, and by Friday they showed great improvement in this area. After all of the readiness preparations for the choral reading, each child was given his booklet and shown how to use the enclosed marker to follow along in reading.

On Monday it seemed that it would be impossible for the children to do choral reading. Through daily work on the program, however, the children did so well by Friday that a tape recording of their performance was made. The following selections were taped: "Quiet Please," "The Wind," "Sneezing," "Jump or Jiggle," and "White Sheep, White Sheep" (Clouds).*

Activities from Poetry

1. Colored books were made from the inspiration gained from "White Sheep, White Sheep." The children formed clouds out of cotton and pasted them on the front of their booklets. Inside they drew pictures of what the clouds looked like to them. I circulated among the children, writing on cards their dictated sentences about the pictures. Each one copied his own original sentence in his book. The children were encouraged to write on their own, spelling words like they sounded to them, but most were reluctant to try since this was their first experience.

2. "Jump or Jiggle" is a wonderful poem made up of kernel sentences about animals. In addition to using it in choral reading, it was used as a basis for selecting an animal to make. For this purpose, children chose either a white or brown sack, stuffed and shaped it with newspaper, tied off its head with yarn or string, added tails with crepe paper, etc. A simple demonstration was given them as to how one could make a mouse. After completing this activity, writing paper was given the children to see if they could tell what they had made. The children wanted so much to cooperate with the writing. Many obtained books and their teacher and I were led to believe they were only looking up words about animals. We soon found they were simply copying from books sentences that had no meaning to the project at hand. After finding this out I decided a different kind of word study

---

* One little boy, who was an expert in "organic" language, could be heard throughout the week as he worked in various activities saying to himself over and over, "White Sheep, white sheep, on a blue hill!" The principal, hearing him, expressed her amazement at such language from this child.

should be started—one that would lead to more independence in writing.

3. Word study was developed from the kernel sentences in "Jump or Jiggle."

It was decided that the kernel sentences the children were beginning to read chorally would be used for word study, sentence expansion, and manuscript writing, simultaneously. Thus, nine kernel sentences were placed on the board a little above the child's eye level. Example: "frogs jump," "bugs wiggle," "rabbits hop," "horses clop." All consonant letters were underlined to emphasize the sound they represent.

Lines were ruled off beneath each kernel sentence so that three children could take their turns at the board under each, thus serving three different teams. The children were instructed *either* to put a *describing word before* the two-word kernel sentence or *to add words* telling *how* or *where.* They each were encouraged to think of something different from what the other children had written. By the second day of this activity, the children began being creative and venturing to write words the way they sounded. Their teacher was quite impressed with the results and intends to continue to develop this activity as a basis for getting the children actively involved in transferring sounds to letters.

Making Sequence Books

Each team was instructed to pick up six related pictures and two pieces of construction paper to make a sequence book. The pictures were randomly arranged so that each child would decide in what order they should be placed. The children were instructed to:

1. number the pictures according to the way they wanted to tell their stories.
2. assemble them according to page number.
3. fit the six-page story into the front and back construction paper book cover.
4. sew the left-hand side of the book—using a darning needle threaded with floss.
5. write or dictate a sentence on each page as to what the story was about.

This is an excellent project—but I found the children needed much more readiness in sequence thinking to make it a successful learning experience. They made their books beautifully, but there was little logic to the way they put them together. It showed us that these children had not had enough experience in thinking through situations. Again, this demonstrates that workbook exercises alone may not lead to thinking; that had been the only way these children had done sequence work previously.

Using Darning Needles Threaded with Colored Floss*

This was the first experience the children had had in sewing booklets. It was quite gratifying to see how careful the children were with the equipment. As each team finished sewing, the needles were replaced for the next group to use. *Not one needle was lost,* and no child had to be reminded to return it to the large receptacle where the needles were kept.

Individualized Reading in Teams

In preparation for meeting with the class, I had collected a group of interesting trade books, written at preprimer and primer level, as well as picture books. After introducing them, I placed the books on the library shelf. With the three teams organized (as previously discussed), the children were told to select either these books *or* their regular reader for reading time with me.

There was only time to try the new reading plan on two days. On the second day the children were beginning to catch on and responded better. It was apparent that a much longer period would be needed to show these children that reading independently of the teacher can be fun.

Since I was interested in having a taped sample of each child's reading from a basal he had used, particularly to note intonation patterns, I used the third day's reading period for that purpose. Each was instructed to bring his assigned basal reader to the tape recorder. In listening to the tape afterwards, I discovered that very few children showed that they had done anything more than word by word reading. How different it was when I listened to the choral reading tape! There was expression, enjoyment, and meaning in their combined voices.

Preparing Food with the Children

On three mornings, different teams met with me fifteen minutes ahead of the class and helped prepare a simple breakfast snack. How each team enjoyed setting the table, making carob milk (substitute for

---

* It must be remembered that most children in kindergarten through second grade *cannot* thread darning needles. The teacher must have a large supply of needles—*threaded ahead of time*—with many different colors of floss or yarn.

chocolate), spreading honey on bread, pouring orange juice, carob milk, and distributing raisins!

One team prepared and served popcorn in the afternoon. The children enjoyed cleaning up afterwards as much as preparing the food.

Summary

I wanted the opportunity to work in the inner city to be able to say with authority that of which I was already certain: Children are basically the same wherever they are—inner city, rural or suburban area, or small town. I have now worked with children in all of these areas and find that the same problems exist in all classrooms, regardless of location. All children need to be involved in the learning process, to be given the opportunity to be creative and think for themselves. All children benefit from nutritious food prepared in the classroom.

Aside from proving to my own satisfaction that the above-mentioned techniques are practical, I value above everything else the fine working relationships I was able to develop with dedicated teachers in the inner city. The classroom teacher and I achieved a relationship that made significant exchange of ideas possible. She was able to show me where I fell short in giving sufficiently detailed directions to children; I was able to show her how to involve children actively in the learning process, and how it was possible for her to carry on and perfect what we started in my four and one-half days with her.

Furthermore, I found that most of the teachers at J. School are dissatisfied with the concept of predetermined material to be covered in one year and want to have help in moving toward a curriculum in which children are personally involved. They reinforced my conviction that a system of *uniform* prescribed teaching *unrelated* to the individual child's learning needs, which incorporates rigid homogeneous grouping and a requirement to do work that has no relevancy to the child and grading him on it, produces one of the following results: a poor self-image *or* a decision that learning is unimportant. The overwhelming problems facing our schools today stem mainly from this.

SUCCESSFUL TEACHING OF DISADVANTAGED CHILDREN— REQUISITES OF THE CLASSROOM TEACHER

Simply having a desire to help the disadvantaged child make progress in school is not enough to qualify a teacher for this task. This is of course a prime requirement but must be supplemented by other traits and training. Let's look at them:

1. Patience and a never-failing belief that each child can make progress if enough time is given to finding out how he learns.
2. Firmness! Many a child is disadvantaged because no one has been concerned enough about him to see that he follows through on what he starts. Coddling and inconsistency in managing children has no place in any classroom, for that matter. Creative teaching requires that orderly classroom practices first be established.
3. *Understanding of the ways cognitive skills (the process of knowing) develop.* A teacher must understand the sequences of development that are the basics for intellectual growth, as well as the types of experiences needed for developing each phase. Some children pass through these sequences more quickly than others, but all normal children progress through the same stages. The teacher who is well grounded in these fundamental learning phases for development of the intellectual will be better able to provide necessary experiences for a particular child, relating him to the "rung of the ladder" he has attained. Briefly, the writer will list the stages described by the eminent psychologist Jean Piaget as the basis for intellectual growth:*

Period I   *The sensori-motor* phase (birth to two years). The child's motor activities, starting at birth, develop body reflexes relating to his environment. Kicking, crawling, reaching, touching, and exploring his surroundings in every possible way, he gains "motor meaning" which lays the groundwork for all learning that comes thereafter. Imitation and play are important ingredients of this period. Interference by severe sickness, malnutrition, or limitations in the child's early environment may cause a problem in adequate perceptual-motor coordination needed for formal learning. "Later developments are built upon foundations laid in infancy" (6).

Teachers should be familiar with Newell C. Kephart's program for remediation (4). A child needs a corrective physical exercise program if he has not developed "body image" based upon his discrimination of laterality, e.g., distinction of right from left;

---

*For a more thorough understanding of these stages it is important that the reader do his own research; the sources listed in the bibliography should be studied as a starting point.

or directionality, e.g., awareness of left, right, front, back in the world around him.

Period II   *Pre-operational* phase* (two years to seven years). The essential difference between this period and the sensori-motor period is that now the child "is capable of manipulating symbols that *represent* the environment" (8). For example, *after a child has taken dominion over his motor experiences—internalized them—he is ready to symbolize them with speech.* His ability to talk is developed in relationship to motor manipulation and direct contact with objects in his environment influenced by interaction with members of his family. Language and thought are related to concrete objects and experiences in his environment. Reality can include past, present, and future. Perception of the world about him is being developed. The breadth of his generalizations depends upon the scope of his environment. Interaction with concrete objects (including books) and opportunity to explore them affect his capacity for developing a generalization.

Period III   *Concrete-operational phase* (seven years and above). The child who has had many and varied concrete experiences, including a multitude of sensory and motor activities, *reaches a point where he has the ability to reason from direct experiences.* "Piaget emphasizes that cognitive activity should be carried out in social situations where children are working together, sharing information, and learning to take into account another person's point of view" (10).

Period IV   *Formal-operational phase* (eleven years and above). The adolescent moves into problem solving, classifying, and abstracting. "The *concrete-operational child* always *starts with experience* and makes limited interpolations and extrapolations from the data available to his senses. *The adolescent,* however, *begins with the possible* and then checks various

---

* Piaget has defined an "operation" as "an action that can return to its starting point, and that can be integrated with other actions also possessing this feature of reversibility" (7).

possibilities against memorial representations of past experience, and eventually against sensory feedback from the concrete manipulations that are suggested by his hypotheses (9).

While age specifications have been indicated for each of the above phases of intellectual development described by Piaget, these stages operate in children and adults alike, as they approach new concepts.

4. *Flexibility.* A prescribed rigid curriculum, ineffective with most children, is certainly unsuited for disadvantaged and culturally different children. A teacher must be fully knowledgeable of the goals of the school curriculum for social studies, science, and math for the particular grade. These goals must be translated into what are found to be the interests and concerns of the children. Teachers must be so skilled in language arts that they are able to use relevant subject areas for developing the oral, written, and reading communication skills of the children from living experiences.

5. A teacher must have a thorough knowledge of psycholinguistics in order to understand how a child internalizes language (speech) which is the foundation for development of reading. Children's "in-group" language (nonstandard English) resulting from cultural deprivation or cultural differences is accepted and understood as he comes to school.

Aside from understanding the linguistic principles that operate for all children in learning to talk and later to read, children with nonstandard English dialect present special problems in learning to use the "public" language. Since the "public" language is the unifying speech of our nation (both the spoken and written code) it must be the ultimate goal for the classroom. In order to achieve this goal, the teacher will need to use great skill in developing it with children. While the child's personal language is first accepted *without any question*, the teacher must develop a careful plan which will gradually help him "grow into" the "public" language usage. The plan will be both indirect and direct:

Indirect—Choral speaking and reading of short melodic poetry must be a part of the everyday routine. Poetry with beautiful language patterns should be selected so that the child automatically embraces "life-lifting" language patterns. A teacher will be amazed to find how quickly children begin chanting catchy phrases from the poetry as they work or play.

Direct—The child's native language patterns are analyzed by the teacher to discover the ways that his patterns differ from standard English. It will be easy for the teacher to make this analysis as *dictation is taken from the child in his own language patterns,* with absolutely no comment as to its variance from standard English. If change is to be effected later, it will have to be done without the child feeling that the language of his home is being criticized. In addition to dictation, the child's native language should be taped at regular intervals for analysis.

Attention should be called to the results of a study made by Mildred R. Gladney and Lloyd Leaverton* (3) with Afro-American students (kindergarten—third grade, inclusive) in a low-income ghetto area. They were able to identify four striking differences in verb usage:

a. The verbs *is* and *are* are omitted:
(1) In simple sentences, e.g.,
He my friend.
(2) In sentences using the present participle form, e.g.,
They playing house.
(3) In sentences expressing the future using the verb go, i.e.,
She gon be a nurse when she grow up.

b. One verb form is used for all subjects in the present tense, i.e.,
Chocolate milk look good.
The baby look like he do.
That boy have a piece of bread.

c. One verb form is used for all subjects in the past tense, i.e.,
We was hungry.
Somebody knock that down.
Yesterday I write my name.

d. *Be* is used in place of *is, am* and *are,* and in sentences describing a recurring event, i.e.,
When my mamma be gone, I take care of the babies.
Sometimes he be riding in the alley.
I be scared when it be thundering.

To help children gradually incorporate the correct verb usage patterns, they developed the following sequence for teaching the verb patterns omitted or incorrectly used:

---

* Quotations used with permission of the National Council of Teachers of English.

Unit 1—am, is, are
Unit 2—was, were
Unit 3—"s," "es"
Unit 4—do, does
Unit 5—say, says
Unit 6—have, has
Unit 7—"ed"
Unit 8—be (3)

No effort should be made to begin the direct development and correction of "home-rooted" language *until children feel secure and comfortable in the classroom.* With this atmosphere established, the teacher can initiate a discussion of the different kinds of language people speak with no inference that any particular form of language is incorrect. Attention should be called to the language we hear on television, the language we read in most storybooks, and, for the older children, the language we read in the newspapers. Children can be led to understand that this is the "public" language, the language that is owned by everyone and which creates a common ground of communication for people all over the United States. With this kind of understanding developed inductively, the children can be encouraged to dramatize their own television programs, write their own books and newspapers making use of the *language of the public.* It will come very slowly for some, but with the classroom setting up its own editors to look for correct public usage, the group will take pride in learning to use another form of language as well as their own "everyday talk" (3).

Involving the Children in Preparing Nutritious Food*

The writer feels there are at least three important reasons for the classroom to include activities of this kind daily:

1. Many hyperactive children are deficient in basic nutrients.

2. Many teachers are also deficient in basic nutrients. To be relaxed and patient with children they need to have inner calm that is aided by a good diet.

3. Cooking in the classroom provides experiences for a functional approach to learning, e.g., reading, math.

---

* A teacher must enlist the support of the principal before embarking upon the plan discussed here for cooking in the classroom.

Too many children and teachers have diets overloaded with carbohydrates and unnatural sweets. Many children have breakfasts—*on the run*—consisting of highly advertised prepared cereals that have little nutritional value. To this refined white sugar is added. Toast is made from bread prepared from bleached white flour, devoid of all natural whole grain nutrients.* Usually the toast is spread with jelly made with an abundance of white sugar. *Most teachers do not* eat breakfast before coming to school. Coffee and doughnuts in the teachers' lounge provide their breakfast fare. This is often supplemented at recess time with more coffee and doughnuts! With imagination and planning, based upon nutritional data being made available by the Department of Health, Education, and Welfare and many experts in the field, the classroom can become an exciting laboratory for improving basic diets. Starting the day off with a nutritious breakfast snack will be good for all.

The first question that is most likely to be raised is, who will pay for nutritional cooking in the classroom? Second, what organization is necessary to put it into effect? And thirdly, should it be necessary for a classroom teacher to take on this responsibility? The following will be an attempt to answer these questions.

It is the practice in most public schools (kindergarten—second grade, inclusive) to have a mid-morning snack of either milk or juice and cookies. Parents and/or the government pay for this. This source of money can be redirected. Additionally, Parent-Teacher Associations can be involved in programs which will help them understand updated nutritional programs. P.T.A.s are always anxious to participate in proposals for the betterment of children, and they work diligently to finance many projects. Regardless of these sources of potential support, the program being suggested here will not be that expensive.

It has already been discussed in this chapter that meaningful room management can come from organizing the class into three "friendship" teams. On a rotating basis a team can prepare simple nutritious food for classroom use. If the day is to start with a breakfast snack prepared from whole grains, fruit, and honey, it should be cooked the afternoon before by one team. Another team can have responsibility for serving it when the children arrive at school. Cooked food can be interspersed with more simple food to prepare and serve, e.g., raisins, dates, prunes, served

---

* Processing and refining of grains and sugar can remove important natural vitamins and minerals essential for normal functioning of nerve tissues. It is important to note that the vitamins found in raw and fresh vegetables, fruits, and whole grains *are next to the outer coverings of grains* and *the peelings of fruits and vegetables*. Vitamins are found, also, in the heart of grains and fruits.

with carob milk,* orange juice or unsweetened pineapple juice. Any of these suggested foods can be accompanied with whole wheat or oatmeal bread, spread with honey.

Starting the program will take supervision and ingenuity on the part of the teacher. Details for this will follow later. The teacher's reward will come after the program has been put into operation. Sitting down with the children to eat a breakfast snack at the beginning of the day *and being served by them* has a calming effect upon the whole room. Interacting with children with interesting informal talk while eating sets the proper tone for cooperative sharing and learning throughout the day. The children love cleaning up; the whole operation of eating together and cleaning up will not take more than thirty minutes at the beginning of the day. It will replace the mid-morning snack (requiring about fifteen minutes of classroom time) that so often takes the edge off appetites for the noon lunch. This program will insure that both the teacher and children start the day off nutritiously. Someone may say, what about the child who has already had a well-balanced nutritious breakfast—does he need to eat at the beginning of the morning? If he doesn't need it he will not eat as much as the other children. However, the writer feels that if a canvas were actually made of what children and teachers eat for breakfast, the deficient breakfast described in the beginning of this section would be found to operate in over half the sample. With a program of this sort in operation, hopefully, hyperactive children who are being given drugs to quiet them can build their bodies nutritiously so the drugs can be abandoned.

Equipment and Supplies Needed for Classroom Cooking

For a class of thirty children the following will be needed:

Electrical Equipment
   Two electric fry pans
   Three electric blenders
   One electric corn popper
Other Equipment
   Measuring cups—eight and sixteen ounce size
   Measuring spoons—all sizes

---

* Carob, from the fruit of the carob tree, has been a source of nutrition for centuries. Carob is high in B vitamins—thiamine and niacin. These vitamins are necessary for proper digestion of carbohydrates, essential for supplying healthy nerves. Since many children are allergic to chocolate, carob will substitute for it and provide the same taste. Children should be encouraged to do research on carob and chocolate.

Stirring spoons (large), can later be used as serving spoons

Large mixing bowls—at least six, can later be used as serving bowls

Four wooden cutting boards

Six medium-sized cutting knives—six inch blade with a handle approximately three and one-half inches long

Individual bowls, cups or glasses, spoons, knives, and napkins*

Honey jar dispensers

Basic Food Supplies

Peanut oil

Whole grain brown rice

Raisins, dates, apples, prunes, bananas

Cinnamon

Honey

Powdered skim milk

Carob

Rolled Oats

Roman Meal cereal

100% whole wheat bread as needed

Popcorn

Salt (sea salt, if possible)

Wheat germ

Examples of Simple Recipes that Children Can Make**

Apple Delight

8 (8-ounce) cups of sliced unpeeled cooking apples

½ cup of raisins (soaked in two cups of water for two hours or more)

1 teaspoon of salt

2 teaspoons of cinnamon

⅔ cup of peanut oil

---

* If the school has a cafeteria it should be possible to borrow needed equipment for eating the breakfast snack. The used dishes and silverware would be returned to the school kitchen for washing. Otherwise it would be advisable to use throw-away paper and plastic equipment. Needed sterilization of individually used dishes and silverware in the classroom will pose too great a problem. However, children can wash the equipment used in preparing the food in the classroom.

** Teachers who do not feel that they would want to have a daily program of cooking in the classroom will find the recipes and planning in this section helpful for occasional use. The discussion of nutritious food should be helpful to a unit study on nutrition and some of the recipes might be tried as a culminating activity.

2 cups of rolled oats
1 cup of honey

Since apples are to be used with skin left on, they must be thoroughly washed and rinsed* before slicing. Cut apples in quarters and remove core from each of the four sections. Place each quarter on cutting board and cut into thin slices. (Children must be taught to direct the cutting knife through apple to cutting board so as not to cut themselves. The writer has found that this task is not too difficult for most first grade children after careful instruction.) Fill the measuring cup to the brim with sliced apples. While apples are being prepared by one-half of the team, the other half can mix together the rolled oats, salt, cinnamon, soaked raisins and honey. The electric fry pan should be preheated to 350 degrees. When the apples are ready place the peanut oil in the fry pan first, then the apples and 8 ounces of water. Over this pour the rest of the ingredients and cover with lid to cook. It may be necessary to reduce the heat to prevent sticking. Stir occasionally. When apples are tender (about fifteen minutes) the Apple Delight is ready to store for the next morning breakfast snack! No refrigeration is needed for overnight. This recipe will make approximately *fifteen* six-ounce *servings*. A small amount of milk can be poured over each serving. A sprinkling of wheat germ on each serving will make it even more nutritious.

Rice-Raisin Pudding

1 cup of whole grain brown rice
3 cups of water
1 cup of raisins
⅔ cup of honey
½ teaspoon of salt
1 teaspoon of cinnamon

Put all in a pan together. Soak for three or four hours. Bring to a boil. Turn heat down so the pudding will cook *very* slowly. It will need to cook *at least* one hour. Stir every so often while cooking. Store for the following morning snack— it needs no refrigeration. This recipe will serve ten. It can be served with milk poured over it.

---

* Organic cleansers safe for washing sprayed fruits and vegetables are available. Because of its organic composition, any cleaning residue left on the washed food is not harmful (toxic) to the body.

For variations in hot morning breakfast snacks, rolled oats or Roman Meal are good substitutes. These should be measured out the afternoon before into the electric frying pan. For each recipe add a cup of raisins and honey to soak overnight with the other ingredients. Ten minutes morning cooking in the classroom, stirring occasionally, will have the cereal hot, ready to serve.

Food for Special Occasions in the Classroom

Holidays, particularly Halloween and birthdays, are usually celebrated in the classroom with food treats. These treats however, too often consist mostly of candy. Children love to pop corn, and popcorn serves as a good natural food substitute and will not cause the over stimulation that often results from the refined sugar in candy. Also, sunflower seeds* make delightful nutritious snacks. Once tried, they become a favorite with children. These special occasions are a good time to use carob powder to take care of the desire for chocolate. Using the electric blender for mixing, children can measure out the ingredients and have a delicious wholesome drink and/or pudding for their celebration.

Carob Milk

6 tablespoons carob powder
4 tablespoons honey
1⅓ cup of powdered milk
5 cups of water
dash of salt

Carob-Banana Pudding

6 very ripe large bananas cut into small pieces
6 tablespoons of powdered milk
6 rounded teaspoons of carob powder

Put one-half cup water in blender before adding the bananas. No cooking is necessary. Nuts may be added.

These recipes can each be made in one blender and will provide ten servings. The Carob-Banana Pudding should be made a few hours ahead of serving; it will taste better if it is cold.

If the classroom has access to an oven, cookies and cake can be made substituting rolled oats for flour, honey for sugar, peanut oil or safflower oil for shortening, and carob powder for chocolate. The following cookie recipe was made by a seven year old:

* The sunflower, named for its face that follows the sun, provides ample interest for art and bird study.

Oatmeal-Carob cookies

1 C. oatmeal
1 C. Whole wheat flour
2 T carob powder (chocolate
                      substitute)
1/2 t salt
2 t. cinnamon
2 T corn oil
2 T Grandma's molasses
2 T honey
1/4 c raisins
1/4 dates
A few peanuts
Mix together and bake on
cooky sheet at 350° 15 min.

by
Sheryl M. Tyree
age 7

As seen in all of the recipes, honey is used as the sweetener. For children to make the transfer from food sweetened with refined white sugar, harmful to their bodies and teeth, they will need more honey at first. The amount can be decreased later. A study of bees and how they make honey can become the basis for a relevant unit study. Children will enjoy reading chorally the following poem:

Honey

Fuzz on bees
Flowering trees
Not a breeze.

Bees in flight
Hive in sight
Honey tonight.

To the soul, sweet
To the bones, meat
To the home, treat.

Norman V. Tyree

They also should be encouraged to write their own poetry about bees. Introducing the format of Haiku poetry* would be appropriate at this point.

Classroom Aides to Assist in Cooking Projects

In the initial organization for classroom cooking, the teacher may feel a definite need for assistance. This assistance can come from such sources as:

1. Students from the fifth- or sixth-grade rooms. This would prove to be a particularly good experience for an underachieving child in reading or math who needs concrete experiences such as would be provided by reading recipes and helping children measure the ingredients needed.

2. Parent assistance—scheduled for an hour daily in the afternoon:
   a) Buy needed supplies for cooking
   b) Work with team preparing food

The teacher would want to be certain that assistants understood that their job was supervisory only; primary grade children can become self-reliant in simple cooking projects. The writer has supervised first and second grade children in making all of the recipes suggested in this chapter. The functional learning of reading and math will be developed with primary grade children *only* as *they read* the simple recipes and gain concrete experiences with the concept of quantity while measuring, counting, and mixing the ingredients.

Parent Involvement in Curriculum Goals

Children who are culturally different, culturally disadvantaged or who have a learning disability of any kind, nonetheless, *have parents who are concerned over their welfare.* The parents who are not are in the minority. Success in reaching classroom goals depends to a large extent upon parents' understanding and participating in formulating

---

* Format for Haiku poetry:
   1. Entire poem written with only seventeen syllables: first line—five syllables, second line—seven syllables, and third line—five syllables.
   2. The lines may rhyme, but it is not necessary. Writing Haiku is like painting a picture to fit a frame of a certain size, shape, and color.
This is an excellent exercise to use to test a child's ability to hear and count parts of words, a prerequisite for developing syllabication skills needed in advanced reading.

them. If parents are to reinforce *at home* what is done in the school, they must be acquainted with classroom goals and the procedures used for their accomplishment. Whenever possible they should be used as aides on a limited basis to assist the classroom teacher.

Developing a cooperative working relationship with parents will be difficult to accomplish in communities where parents are culturally different or culturally disadvantaged. These parents are both proud and insecure. To succeed with them, it will be necessary for the teacher to become acquainted with the culture and dialect of the school community. Successful classroom learning will build upon the mores, aspirations, and strengths of the community. The writer cannot prescribe how this is to be done; *this is the responsibility of the ingenious teacher* who has classroom goals meaningful to a particular community. It will involve frequent informal meetings with parents where the climate is conducive to their participation. Perhaps as a starter, in grades one through three, nonworking mothers could be invited to the classroom for the last hour of the school day. Simple nutritious refreshments made and served by the children could create the atmosphere for joint planning later.

In order for mothers to attend, preschool children will have to be invited. Provision for their care can be cooperatively planned with the principal, kindergarten, and upper grade teachers.* Children in upper grades will be needed for aides during that hour. In addition, parents who do not attend should be individually contacted so that they also may understand the goals of the classroom. *This has to be worked at but can be accomplished!*

Teachers must accept their responsibility as interpreters of curriculum in relationship to child growth, e.g., how a child learns to read. As parents gain more understanding, a more relaxed situation will result in the home. When undue pressures at home are removed, children will respond more quickly in school. Parents need to know in what ways they can reinforce classroom practices.

Using Parents as Aides

There will be a few parents from each class who will have the time, desire, and ability to assist the teacher with certain classroom tasks, such as:

1. Type stories for bookmaking

---

* Separate facilities such as the kindergarten room, gym, or any other available room should be provided for the care of the preschool children.

2. Stitch inside pages on sewing machine for children's individual stories (See instruction for bookmaking in appendix.)
3. Assist with classroom cooking projects
4. Contact other parents about school meetings for cooperative planning

Many more tasks are suitable for parent assistance which will provide the teacher with more time for individual instruction of children. Also, many parents as well as other members of the community have talents that should be used to enrich the curriculum. As the school, the parents, and the community are brought together in a meaningful working relationship, the schools will better serve children. Without such cooperation the schools will fail.

REFERENCES

1. Ashton-Warner, Sylvia. *Teacher.* New York: Bantam Publishing Co., 1963.

2. Black, Millard H. "Beginning Reading Programs for the Culturally Disadvantaged." *First Grade Reading Programs.* Edited by James F. Kerfoot. Newark, Delaware: International Reading Association, 1967, p. 165.

3. Gladney, Mildred R., and Leaverton, Lloyd. "A Model for Teaching Standard English to Non-Standard English Speakers." *Elementary English.* Urbana, Illinois: National Council of Teachers of English, October 1968, pp. 758-763.

4. Kephart, N. C. *The Slow Learner in the Classroom.* Columbus, Ohio: Charles E. Merrill Publishing Co., 1971.

5. Martin, Bill J. "Helping Children Claim Language Through Literature." *Elementary English.* Urbana, Illinois: National Council of Teachers of English, May 1968.

6. Phillips, John L., Jr. *The Origins of Intellect: Piaget's Theory.* San Francisco: W. H. Freeman and Company, 1969, p. 15.

7. Phillips, John L., Jr. *The Origins of Intellect: Piaget's Theory.* San Francisco: W. H. Freeman and Company, 1969, p. 53.

8. Phillips, John L., Jr. *The Origins of Intellect: Piaget's Theory.* San Francisco: W. H. Freeman and Company, 1969, p. 54.

9. Phillips, John L., Jr. *The Origins of Intellect: Piaget's Theory.* San Francisco: W. H. Freeman and Company, 1969, p. 104.

10. Raven, Ronald J., and Salzer, Richard T. *The Reading Teacher.* Newark, Delaware: International Reading Association, April 1971, p. 636.

SUPPLEMENTARY REFERENCES

Coles, Robert, M.D. *Teachers and the Children of Poverty.* Washington, D.C.: The Potomac Institute, Inc., 1970.

Concluding
Summary

Throughout this book suggestions for teaching reading have been based upon linguistic principles:

Keeping the melody of language whole for children through choral reading as they "grow into reading"

Using the phoneme approach (speech to print) in developing the encoding and decoding process

Leading children to make discoveries about language (phonemes, morphemes) *within the framework of language patterns*— absolutely necessary for independent reading

Helping children develop ways of self-expression for oral and written use through sentence expansion

Keeping language natural and meaningful

The success of these five points depends upon relevant classroom experiences every day where each child is personally involved in learning activities and respected for his contribution. *Much* class *discussion* leading to further exploration *will result,* a prerequisite for "growing into reading." There will not be "redbirds," "bluebirds," or "dumbbirds"! The children whose growth patterns are fast will be challenged to work independently within the framework of meaningful classroom units, developing their reading skills through wide independent reading and research. The slower maturing children will make their contribution to the classroom unit by authoring material based upon personal experi-

141

ences relating to the unit. Simple books on the subject under study must be available for them. All children's reading skill development will be constantly strengthened by the many methods suggested throughout the book. Children will be given teacher reinforcement:

Individually through *daily short conferences* to check skills learned
In small *changing* groups for specific skill development
Via headphones, using teacher prepared tapes with written material for the aural-visual assimilation of the code

Children will be helped to organize their own daily time schedules by "signing up" for:

Individual teacher conferences, for reading and short discussions
Use of visual and auditory equipment
Use of designated space for experimentation and purposeful projects

These procedures will help build inner controls within the children necessary for an orderly classroom. Such an atmosphere will *free the teacher to assist* where assistance is needed as children work independently. Time for individual conferences and group instruction will be scheduled easily within this framework.

The end result of such a classroom laboratory environment will be the *preservation* and *extension* of *children's natural inquisitiveness—* while they learn to read as they learned to talk.

How to Make Hard-
Back Books

1. Take 2 pieces of cardboard which are the same size and lay them side by side, leaving about ½ inch of space between them.

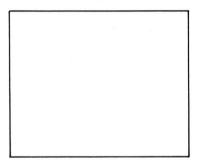

2. Take 4 or 5 pieces of masking tape and run them horizontally across starting at top and bottom of the cardboard, and then 3 or 4 across center.

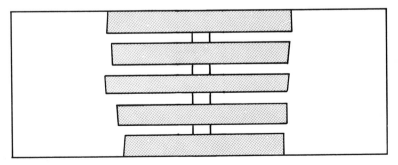

3. Next take 2 long pieces of masking tape and run them vertically between the two pieces of cardboard on the front and back.

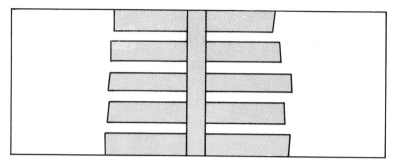

4. Now take material (wallpaper, contact paper, wrapping paper, or whatever you would like for a covering) and cut it to cover the entire cover, leaving an extra inch all around. (Figure A)

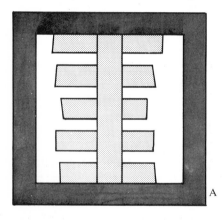
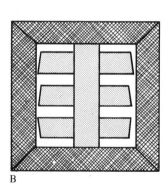

A   B

5. Fold the material down and paste it all around. (Figure B)
6. Fold paper in half for pages.

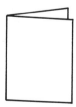

To give the inside a neat, finished look, cut a piece of colored paper for the front and back inside covers, about ¼ inch smaller than the cover. Fold on outside of book pages. The colored paper is sewed with the inside pages.

7. Use an awl to punch holes (½″ apart) through paper for stitching. Place paper on scrap wood to avoid damaging desk.

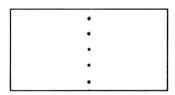

8. a. Cut thread 3½ times the height of the page. Thread a needle.
   b. Knot thread 2″ from end to allow for tying final stitch.
   c. Start stitching from back of book.
      Continue sewing in and out punched holes and you will be surprised to find that when you return to your starting place you now can knot both ends of your thread. A perfect binding is the result.

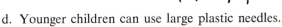

   d. Younger children can use large plastic needles.
   e. These inside pages can be stitched on the sewing machine if the teacher prefers to have them already prepared for the children's use.

9. Corrected stories are either copied by the children on the prepared inside pages or may be typed. Adequate space should be left throughout the booklet for the children's illustrations.

10. After completion of the inside pages use rubber cement on the colored paper to secure the inside pages to the hard-back book covers. With this done the book is completed.

Junction
Box

Headphones

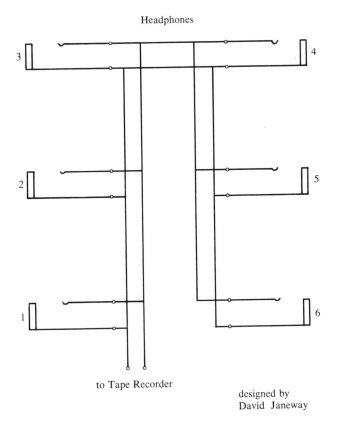

3

4

2

5

1

6

to Tape Recorder

designed by
David Janeway

Parts*	Approximate Cost	
Junction Box	$10.00	
6 Headphones	19.50	@ $3.25 ea.
Patch Cord	3.00	
2 Adapters (optional)	1.25	
to connect record player	Total $33.75	
to junction box		

---

* Parts suggested here are made in Japan. To obtain materials at this price it will be necessary to buy them from electronic equipment distributors. A junction box could be made at less expense by teachers who have ability in assembling electrical equipment: 1 junction enclosure box, $1.00; 1 plug input and wire, $1.00; 6 jacks @ 40¢ each. Thus, $5.00 would cover approximately the total cost. This can be an excellent project for children in the upper grades to make under supervision; or for teachers to make in a workshop.

Information developed with the help of Robert Carter, Academic Media Coordinator, Northern Michigan University.

The Informal
Reading Inventory*

The Informal Reading Inventory (IRI) is an individual diagnostic test. The child reads orally and silently from increasingly difficult material until the material becomes frustrating either in terms of accuracy of pronunciation or understanding of ideas in the content. It is diagnostic in that it reveals for the observant teacher specific areas of difficulty in reading. The Informal Reading Inventory provides a passage of reading at each level from preprimer on until the child's instructional level of reading is found. The child is given a copy of each graded passage; the teacher, likewise, has a copy of each passage being read for marking errors, making notes, and evaluating as the child reads. Mechanical errors to be noted in reading are 1) unknown words,** 2) mispronunciation, 3) insertions, 4) substitutions, 5) omissions.

The *Independent Level of reading* is the level at which the child makes no more than *one error in 100 words* in the mechanics of reading and has no difficulty in comprehension.

The *Instructional Level of reading* is the level at which the child makes no more than five uncorrected errors in reading 100 running words (one word in twenty for shorter passages) and comprehends 75 percent of prepared questions over its content. The *instructional level* of reading is the *teaching level*.

---

* A more accurate appraisal of the child's reading level will result when the tape recorder is used to record oral reading and answers to questions. The child does not "tense up" feeling he is being tested as often happens when he sees the teacher making notations on the record sheet. Furthermore, a teacher may be inaccurate in marking the record while giving the test.

** Supplied by teacher after five seconds of hesitation.

When the total mechanical and comprehension errors are beyond the instructional level, the *Capacity Level*, or *hearing comprehension level* of the child is determined through listening. The child's capacity for understanding ideas when he listens to someone else read the graded material is thus measured. The reading levels with prepared questions become increasingly more difficult. A comprehension score of 75 percent on the prepared questions asked on the material read to him establishes his innate ability to read when he has mastered the decoding skills.

INDEPENDENT LEVEL:

At this level of supplementary reading the child should be able to read the book at home or at school without aid. The material should cause no difficulty and have high interest value. 90% comprehension. 99% pronunciation. No head movements. No finger pointing. No vocalization. Good phrasing.—E. A. Betts

The interpretation of independent reading as a skill permitting wide reading above the grade level of instructional materials is a practical recognition of the relationship of pupil interest and silent-reading abilities. . . . When reading interest is strong, the exact reading level of a book is not too important, within reasonable limits, so long as the content appeals to the child.—G. D. Spache

INSTRUCTIONAL LEVEL:

This is the highest level at which a child can do satisfactory reading provided that he receives preparation and supervision from a teacher; word recognition errors are not frequent, comprehension and recall are satisfactory.—A. J. Harris

This is the teaching level. The reading material must be challenging and not too difficult. 75% comprehension. 95% pronunciation. No signs of discomfort.—E. A. Betts

---

Betts, Emmet, *Foundations of Reading Instruction* (New York: American Book Company, 1950).

Spache, George D., *Reading in the Elementary School* (Boston: Allyn and Bacon, Inc. 1964).

Harris, A. J., *How to Increase Reading Ability*, 4th ed. (New York: David McKay, 1961).

Index

Index